Xamarin.Forms Essentials

First Steps Toward Cross-Platform Mobile Apps

Gerald Versluis

Xamarin.Forms Essentials

Gerald Versluis
Sittard, The Netherlands

ISBN-13 (pbk): 978-1-4842-3239-2   ISBN-13 (electronic): 978-1-4842-3240-8
https://doi.org/10.1007/978-1-4842-3240-8

Library of Congress Control Number: 2017961816

Cover image designed by Freepik

Managing Director: Welmoed Spahr
Editorial Director: Todd Green
Acquisitions Editor: Jonathan Gennick
Development Editor: Laura Berendson
Coordinating Editor: Jill Balzano
Copy Editor: Kezia Endsley
Compositor: SPi Global
Indexer: SPi Global
Artist: SPi Global

Distributed to the book trade worldwide by Springer Science+Business Media New York, 233 Spring Street, 6th Floor, New York, NY 10013. Phone 1-800-SPRINGER, fax (201) 348-4505, e-mail orders-ny@springer-sbm.com, or visit www.springeronline.com. Apress Media, LLC is a California LLC and the sole member (owner) is Springer Science + Business Media Finance Inc (SSBM Finance Inc). SSBM Finance Inc is a **Delaware** corporation.

For information on translations, please e-mail rights@apress.com, or visit http://www.apress.com/rights-permissions.

Apress titles may be purchased in bulk for academic, corporate, or promotional use. eBook versions and licenses are also available for most titles. For more information, reference our Print and eBook Bulk Sales web page at http://www.apress.com/bulk-sales.

Any source code or other supplementary material referenced by the author in this book is available to readers on GitHub via the book's product page, located at www.apress.com/9781484232392. For more detailed information, please visit http://www.apress.com/source-code.

Printed on acid-free paper

Table of Contents

About the Author

 **Gerald Versluis** is a full-stack software developer and Microsoft MVP from The Netherlands. He has many years of experience working with .NET technologies, Azure, and Xamarin. Gerald has been involved in a variety of roles in numerous projects. A great number of these projects involve developing Xamarin apps. Not only does Gerald like to code, but he also is keen on spreading his knowledge and gaining some in the bargain. Gerald speaks, records vlogs, provides training sessions, and writes blogs and articles in his spare time.

Acknowledgments

I want to thank Jonathan for his belief in me and for encouraging me to write another book this quickly. Also, Jill, again thanks for the great collaboration.

Also, thank you dear Laurie for (again) being patient and supportive and for believing in me while I put a lot of time and effort in this book.

And of course, I want to thank you, the reader holding this book right now, for reading! You are the ones I am doing this for, so I hope this book met your expectations and that you have found it useful to make you a better professional. May this book help you put together awesome apps!

Introduction

While I was planning on doing a second book, I didn't plan on it to come this fast. My first book just came out earlier this year and I still have this magical smile whenever I hold a copy in my hand. And now there already is a second!

I wanted to do another book, mainly because I love help starting developers begin their journeys. With this book, I hope you will learn what Xamarin as a company is all about and why I love Xamarin.Forms as a technique.

By using a real-life app that is available in the app stores right now as an example, I hope I can make the concepts of Xamarin.Forms as clear as possible. What I have learned from writing this book is that it's hard to put on paper what you mean by a certain piece of code. By referring to code in the sample app and being able to try the functionality yourself, I've made it as clear as possible.

If anything isn't clear or you have any questions or comments, please don't hesitate to reach out to me. I love to hear from my readers and see what they've created.

Have a blast reading this book; I know I have enjoyed writing it.

PART I

What Is Xamarin.Forms?

CHAPTER 1

A Brief History of Xamarin

Before you start diving into the specifics of Xamarin.Forms, it will be useful for you to have a little more information about Xamarin itself. This chapter explains where Xamarin came from, where it is now, and why there was a need for Xamarin.Forms to begin with. In addition, it shows you what is contained in Xamarin.Forms and when to use it or when to avoid it. For brevity, you may find that I simply use the term "Forms" instead of the full Xamarin.Forms name.

How It All Started

Xamarin.Forms is only a small part of the greater solution that is called Xamarin. Xamarin is both the name of the technique and the name of the company that is behind it. But before it became the company as we know it, there has been a lot going on.

It all started with Miguel de Icaza and Nat Friedman, both still heavily involved. They founded a company together in 1999, which eventually will be known as Ximian. At that time, they were focused on developing GNOME, which is a desktop environment for Unix-based systems.

Soon after Microsoft announced the .NET Framework in June 2000, Miguel started investigating whether a Linux counterpart would be possible. This led to the launch of the Mono project in July 2001. This open

© Gerald Versluis 2017

G. Versluis, *Xamarin.Forms Essentials*, https://doi.org/10.1007/978-1-4842-3240-8_1

source project is basically the foundation of Xamarin. Back in 2001, the goal was set to run .NET Framework applications on other platforms.

In 2003, Novell acquired Ximian, along with the Mono project. Novell was known for being one of the first companies that facilitated thin clients, by being able to run applications on the server. The acquisition of Ximian was the start of transitioning their product suite to a Linux base.

After three years of development, major version 1.0 of the Mono project was released in 2004. This was only a year before Microsoft released version 2.0 of the .NET Framework. As you may recall, Microsoft did not support the open source idea back then. Because of that, support for Mono would always be behind the implementation of Microsoft, and as time passed, this gap was quickly closed. However, some form of collaboration happened and was further expanded in 2006. During the time that Ximian was under the care of Novell, Mono did not live up to its potential.

After a lot of hard work in 2009, Mono Touch, the foundation of Xamarin as a technology, was released. With the release of Mono Touch 1.0, C# applications could be submitted to the iOS app store. Actually, at some point around the iOS 4 release in 2010, there was a little dispute on Apple banning Mono Touch applications (along with Flash) from the app store. Apple updated their license agreement with:

> *"Applications may only use documented APIs in the manner prescribed by Apple and must not use or call any private APIs. Applications must be originally written in Objective-C, C, C++, or JavaScript as executed by the iPhone OS WebKit engine, and only code written in C, C++, and Objective-C may compile and directly link against the documented APIs (e.g., applications that link to documented APIs through an intermediary translation or compatibility layer or tool are prohibited)."*

This meant that all cross-compiled apps would not be allowed, including Mono Touch applications. The main reason would be that Apple would lose control over the ecosystem they had created. After a lot of criticism, the rules were toned down a little, allowing other programming languages to be used. However, as a side note, you still need Mac hardware to compile your iOS applications.

Also in 2010, Novell was acquired by a company called Attachmate. In April 2011, most of the Novell team was laid off. This begged the question of what would happen to the Mono project. And more importantly for mobile developers, what would happen to the Mono Touch project.

Soon after the layoffs, in a blog post, Miguel announced that Mono would find continuation in a newly founded company called Xamarin. Nat Friedman was appointed the CEO of Xamarin soon after.

If you have ever wondered where the name Xamarin came from, consider what Miguel de Icaza said in an interview with `adtmag.com`: (see `https://adtmag.com/blogs/watersworks/2011/05/interview-with-miguel-de-icaza.aspx`):

> *"We've used monkey themes for many years," de Icaza said. "Ximian was a play on simian. Mono is Spanish for monkey. Xamarin comes from the Tamarin monkey. And we kept the X; though to tell you the truth, I can't remember why we used it in the first place."*

Xamarin Today

The rest is history, as they say. From the launch of Xamarin as a company, things started to accelerate. In 2012 and 2013, it went a bit silent, but Xamarin introduced their flagship products. Xamarin.Mac, released in December 2012, enabled developers to write C# applications for the MacOS desktop. In February 2013, Xamarin.iOS and Xamarin.Android were released. At this time, developers could share code between iOS, Android, and MacOS. Implicitly Windows Phone, released in October of 2012, was supported as well, because this was already based on C# and .NET technology.

Along with the Xamarin framework, Xamarin Studio was also released. This Integrated Development Environment (IDE) would be *the* choice for developing Xamarin cross-platform apps for several years to come.

In the meantime, Microsoft was changing course rapidly as well. A lot of the .NET projects were converted to open source and put on GitHub. Windows Phone was still being maintained, but the future of it seems unsure. Certainly, with the introduction of Universal Windows Platform (UWP) apps, it is now possible to run your app on any Windows-based device, including but not limited to Xbox, HoloLens, Windows Phone, and Windows 10 desktop.

In February 2016, the whole Xamarin crew became part of Microsoft. Not long after that, more good news was in store. At the Build conference, Microsoft announced that the Xamarin development tools would be free and become open source as well.

With the acquisition of Xamarin, Microsoft is a contender in the mobile market. Before, they had a hard time gaining some market share with the Windows Phone, but now they have a full end-to-end C# solution for developing applications. And not just developing!

In December 2014, Microsoft bought HockeyApp, a solution for crash reporting, analytics, and distribution of mobile apps. HockeyApp, Xamarin, and what Microsoft already had in their portfolio combined, makes them the most complete vendor for everything mobile to date as far as I am concerned.

As to be expected, some Xamarin branded components are being replaced slowly by the Microsoft brand. Xamarin Studio is now Visual Studio for Mac with more Azure options; the Xamarin MVP program is fused with the Microsoft MVP program; etc. But I think it will take a while before the name Xamarin will disappear completely, at least at the company level.

But it doesn't stop at rebranding. Microsoft is also putting a lot of effort into bringing all the acquired solutions together and introduced Mobile Center in November 2016. This user-friendly environment combines all the best parts of Visual Studio Team Services (VSTS), Xamarin Test Cloud, and HockeyApp, as well as some parts of Azure relevant to mobile into a single point of entry. While still in preview at the time of writing, there is a lot you can do already. Just before the release of this book Microsoft has taken Mobile Center out of preview. It is now called App Center. Where

I write Mobile Center in the remainder of this book, I actually mean App Center. The functionalities should be identical or by the time you're reading this will even be expanded.

Tip   If you want to read more on building your apps with VSTS, Mobile Center, or using Xamarin Test Cloud, which we cover in a bit, you can take a look at my other book I have written on this subject, entitled *Xamarin Continuous Integration and Delivery: Team Services, Test Cloud, and HockeyApp*, which you can find at `https://www.amazon.com/Xamarin-Continuous-Integration-Delivery-HockeyApp/dp/1484227158`.

Near the end of this book, we will look ahead to the things that are coming in regards to Xamarin and cross-platform development.

Product Suite

So you can get a better understanding of Xamarin as a whole, this section summarizes all the relevant products with brief descriptions of each.

Xamarin Platform

The main product is of course the whole Xamarin platform. Released with Xamarin 2.0 in February 2013, Xamarin Platform enabled developers to write cross-platform applications with Visual Studio or Xamarin Studio. Supported platforms at that time were iOS, Android, Windows, and Mac. Today, there are a lot more platforms supported and a lot more to come.

Xamarin.Forms

As part of the Xamarin platform, Xamarin.Forms was introduced in May 2014. I won't spoil too much here, as we will go into this subject in the next chapter and for the remainder of this book.

Xamarin Test Cloud

Another unique service from the Xamarin minds is Xamarin Test Cloud. Test Cloud is a service for automated UI testing of your apps. And not just Xamarin apps either—native and hybrid apps are supported as well!

The services that Test Cloud offers are quite unique. You can write coded UI tests, which run on actual *physical* devices. This way, you get as close to a user experience as you can get. You do not have to buy a lot of expensive hardware. Test Cloud has over 2500 unique configurations at the time of writing, with about a 100 added each month alone. The results are conveniently shown in a great interface, complete with screenshots and logging, as shown in Figure 1-1. To read more on Xamarin Test Cloud, visit `https://www.xamarin.com/test-cloud`.

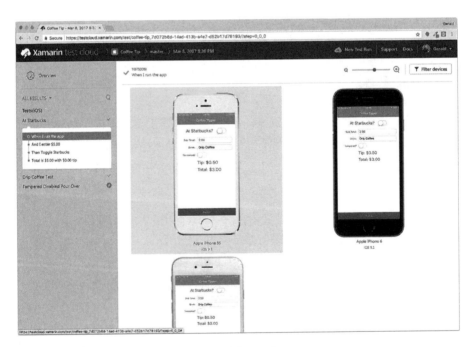

Figure 1-1. *Test Cloud result dashboard*

Under the Test Cloud umbrella is the Test Recorder, which lets you record tests with an easy-to-user interface.

Xamarin Studio/Visual Studio for Mac

Based on MonoDevelop, Xamarin Studio was an IDE specifically designed for cross-platform development. This lightweight application had all the basic features of its big brother Visual Studio. After Microsoft acquired Xamarin, Xamarin Studio quickly became Visual Studio for Mac. The initial version wasn't more than a rebrand with some Azure shortcuts, but as the time passes and the development of .NET Standard and .NET Core are progressing, it is turning into a full-featured IDE.

Xamarin for Visual Studio

It is almost easy to forget that support for Xamarin in Visual Studio (for Windows) doesn't come naturally. What began as a (very extensive) plugin has become a first-class citizen of the Visual Studio development suite. It supports everything that one might wish for in cross-platform development. As part of Xamarin for Visual Studio, there are a lot of products.

- **Mac build host**: You still need Mac hardware to compile your iOS apps. To accommodate for this, Xamarin has developed an agent that you can run on your Mac and that communicates with Visual Studio. This way, your app is compiled on the Mac, but all the results, debugging, etc. can happen on your Windows machine.

- **Remoted iOS Simulator**: Together with the Mac build host, this makes developing on Windows possible. With the Remoted iOS Simulator, the iOS Simulator can be shown on a Windows environment. The Simulator, part of Apple's IDE Xcode, only runs on a Mac, but Xamarin has found a way to mirror the display of the Simulator to Windows. This means developers don't have to switch between machines while working on their apps. To learn more about the Remoted Simulator, visit `https://developer.xamarin.com/guides/cross-platform/windows/ios-simulator/`.

- **Xamarin Profiler**: An application with which an app can be profiled. You can inspect its memory usage as well as call trees and other advanced stuff. With this product, you can really polish and optimize your app, but be warned—it is pretty advanced stuff! If you want to know more, you can read it at `https://www.xamarin.com/profiler`.

Xamarin Workbooks

One more notable product is the Xamarin Workbooks, which is kind of a standalone product. While it is invented by the Xamarin team, it doesn't just target Xamarin development. You can use it with all kinds of .NET-related technologies.

The goal of Workbooks is to blend code with documentation. Because of that, it can be used in a wide variety of ways. Think of interactive learning guides, education, experimentation, etc.

With Markdown—a way of styling text through common characters—you can format text to describe to the reader what your goal is. With the tight integration with Roslyn, which is basically a compiler as a service, code can be executed inline and the results are visible instantly. It also has IntelliSense support and other features. In Figure 1-2, you can see an example of such a Workbook in action, but it is self-explanatory if you start playing around with it.

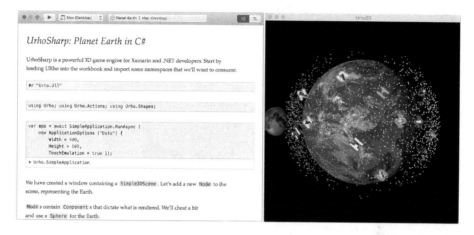

Figure 1-2. *A Xamarin Workbook in action, explaining UrhoSharp*

For more information on Workbooks, refer to `https://developer.xamarin.com/guides/cross-platform/workbooks/`.

I am probably forgetting some other larger or smaller products, but this is the gist of it. I hope you can see that Xamarin is so much more than just the cross-platform development. While that is the focus on nearly all of the products, there are a lot of awesome tools in this toolbelt.

The Xamarin Vision

This section elaborates a bit more on the vision and unique approach of Xamarin. I do this by explaining a bit more about development before Xamarin and how they are achieving cross-platform development today. That way, you will have a better understanding of the inner workings of Xamarin and Xamarin.Forms.

Before Xamarin, there was the traditional approach of developing native apps. Xamarin likes to call this the "silo" approach. This is shown in Figure 1-3.

Silo Approach

iOS	Android	Windows
Objective-C Swift Xcode	Java Android Studio	C# Visual Studio

No shared code | Multiple languages & development ecosystems | multiple teams

Figure 1-3. *The silo approach means building one app three times*

You had to build your app over and over, for each platform you wanted to support. Each app would, ideally, have the same features, but each was built in its own programming language, in its own IDE. It is not very likely that one person can have perfect knowledge of all these ecosystems, so the silo approach most likely needs multiple teams.

You can see why this has several disadvantages. It costs a lot of time and money to keep all these apps at the same level of functionalities. Also, tests will not be interchangeable, so testing also costs three times as much. And worst of all, you can have different bugs on different platforms. I didn't even mention the hardware and licenses you would have to buy to support all this development.

If I would have to name one advantage of the silo approach, it is that because each app is written in its own language, the performance should be the best of all approaches. Notice how I am saying *should*. There are benchmarks that show that Xamarin is marginally faster than native development tools. There are multiple benchmarks out there, but I like the ones by Harry Cheung, former Google engineer. You can read his posts here: `https://medium.com/@harrycheung/cross-platform-mobile-performance-testing-d0454f5cd4e9` and the updated post here: `https://medium.com/@harrycheung/mobile-app-performance-redux-e512be94f976`.

The next approach is the hybrid approach, also known as "Write Once, Run Anywhere". Think of solutions like PhoneGap and Ionic. These frameworks mostly allow developers to start off relatively easy, because they are based on web technology. So, you can start writing your app very quickly using HTML and JavaScript or Lua, etc. Figure 1-4 illustrates this concept.

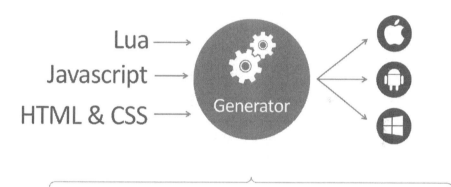

Figure 1-4. *The hybrid approach*

This way of developing means that you are mostly limited to the APIs that are the common denominator on all platforms. Each phone has a camera nowadays, so that is supported. Not all phones have augmented reality features, so to support that from day one, you have to write Java or Objective-C code. Also, the render time tends to be slower. Even worse, when your CSS fails to load, your user is presented with an ugly app, leaving them puzzled.

Most of the time, hybrid apps also look the same across all platforms. While that seems convenient from a developer's perspective, from a user perspective, it is not. I will elaborate more on that in a minute when I explain the Xamarin approach.

All in all, the hybrid approach seems to cause more misery than anything else. In all fairness, I haven't touched any hybrid development solutions in-depth. But I can usually pick out the hybrid apps from the store, and not in a good way.

All of this raises the question: what is native? We often hear that native apps are best. But what does *native* mean? That is what the people at Xamarin asked themselves before setting out on their journey.

They came up with the following characteristics:

- *Looks and feels like it belongs on that platform.* The app should adopt the paradigm of the platform it's running on. Adhere to the navigation pattern, have controls that the user is used to from other apps, and so on. Remember when I spoke of the generic look and user experience for apps with the hybrid approach? That is what you want to avoid. When the look and feel does not comply with the rest of the ecosystem, the user will be confused.

- *100% API access.* The developer should have access to all of the APIs that are available on that platform. No exceptions. When some new awesome feature is announced for the new iOS, you must be able to use it in your app. And not just the Apple or Google APIs either, you must also be able to use any third-party API and library out there.

- *Provides the best performance.* It must provide the best performance. Although it may not be the native programming language, the app still must be responsive and fast.

These days, users have high expectations! When your app is not doing what it should, it is usually uninstalled within 30 seconds and it will be really hard to convince the user to come back after that. So, these statements about what is native are important.

With that in mind, Xamarin came up with their own approach to things, as shown in Figure 1-5.

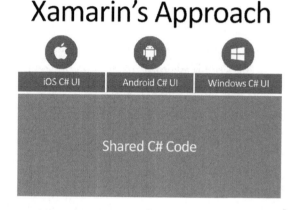

Figure 1-5. The Xamarin approach to cross-platform development

Xamarin basically created mappings for all native APIs and made them available through C# and .NET. In fact, it makes perfect sense, because Microsoft has been doing this for years. Whenever you started a WinForms project, you would get the base .NET Framework libraries, with a set specific to WinForms as an addition. Planning on an ASP.NET application? You get the same set of base libraries and a specific set to ASP.NET.

The team at Xamarin created so-called projections. Each method, object, property, etc. that is available in Objective-C of Java Xamarin is available in .NET with its own types. That way everything is available to the developers, most of the time from day one.

Especially for iOS, Xamarin has an unbeaten track record since iOS 5. The day that Apple releases the new (final) iOS version, Xamarin has updated their bits, and everything is available to you as well. For iOS, this is important, because the adoption rate on a new iOS version is quite high. On Android, not so much. Months after an update is released, people are still stuck on the older version. So, the same-day support isn't as relevant. That does not mean that Xamarin is lacking with adding new APIs. Although it may not be the same day, it is soon after release. If you miss anything, like support for some third-party library, Xamarin has you covered. The tools that are used internally to create the projections are available to you as well. That way, you can create your own binding library for a native API if you want to.

The statement Xamarin has always carried out is the following:

"Anything you can do in Objective-C, Swift, or Java can be done in C# and Visual Studio with Xamarin."

I still haven't found anything to counter that statement.

When Microsoft took over, things went a step further. With developments like .NET Core and .NET Standard, cross-platform development is looking better than ever before. This enables developers to develop code that is truly useable across platforms. In Figure 1-6, you can see an example of that.

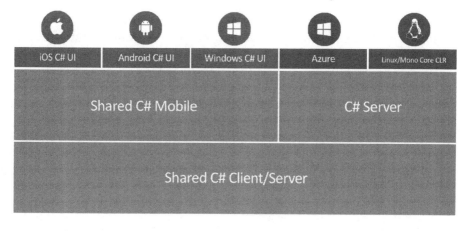

Figure 1-6. *Example of an architecture with end-to-end C# code*

I'd like to end this chapter with the new mantra that Microsoft is now putting on the Xamarin branch:

"Any Developer, Any App, Any Platform"

I love it!

Summary

I hope you enjoyed reading this chapter as much as I did writing it. Although I only did a quick recap of all the facts, it is an absolute joy to read this story. A lot of things had to go right (or wrong, depending on where you're standing) to make all of this happen and put Xamarin where it is in the world today. Personally, I love the passion of namely Miguel, but also Nat and all the people making this possible and who kept believing in their solution. While it hasn't always been perfect, it was never because of lack of trying. When you realize what Xamarin is trying to do, it's a miracle something works at all. The thing they are trying to do is make all kinds of different Software Development Kits (SDKs) from all types of vendors, each with their own attitude and quirks, work together in one stable, easy-to-use solution. That is hard to maintain when you are so dependent on others all the time.

This works the other way too—make no mistake, mobile development is hard. If you thought .NET exceptions were hard to read, wait until you see some Java ones. And now you do not need to know about one development ecosystem, but three at least. While Xamarin is making it the best they can, it's not always a breeze. Especially when you're just getting started.

The sources I used for this chapters are various, including some stories I picked up in sessions and conversations I had over the years, but also these:

- Strikingly: `http://corefx.strikingly.com/`

- Wikipedia: `https://en.wikipedia.org/wiki/Xamarin`, `https://en.wikipedia.org/wiki/Novell`, `https://en.wikipedia.org/wiki/Miguel_de_Icaza`

- Adtmag.com: `https://adtmag.com/blogs/watersworks/2011/05/interview-with-miguel-de-icaza.aspx`

In this chapter, you learned how Xamarin became Xamarin and where it stands today. It also explained the Xamarin vision and how extensive their suite is. You learned about the landscape of the various mobile development approaches and read about how Xamarin works its magic. This way you will have a better understanding of what is coming in this book.

In the next chapter, I zoom in on Xamarin.Forms specifically. You will see why Xamarin.Forms was necessary to allow for more code sharing and will learn how it works.

CHAPTER 2

Introducing Xamarin.Forms

In this chapter, we look at Xamarin.Forms from a high level. You will learn what the use case is for using Xamarin.Forms and the possibilities when using it. And then there is the question on how to define a layout with Forms—there are two possibilities with very little differences. And lastly, I will go into a bit of the internals of Xamarin.Forms.

The Necessity of Xamarin.Forms

In 2014 Xamarin.Forms as we now know it was added to the Xamarin product suite. With Xamarin it was already possible to write code in C# and run that code across multiple platforms, mainly iOS, Android, and Windows Phone. However, the user interface (UI) code still had to be coded for each separate platform. In this situation, code sharing would only go as high as 80%. The remaining 20% is the UI code that had to be dealt with on a per-platform basis.

This is not necessarily a bad thing. As a developer, you do want to write your code just once, but working on multiple platforms does not mean that your app should look the same across all of these. The users of each respective ecosystem have different expectations in terms of navigation

© Gerald Versluis 2017
G. Versluis, *Xamarin.Forms Essentials*, https://doi.org/10.1007/978-1-4842-3240-8_2

and look-and-feel. As part of the Xamarin toolkit, they had already integrated the iOS and Android designers into Visual Studio and Xamarin Studio. This way it would be easier to design the UI.

But the team at Xamarin wanted more. They wanted to get as close to the 100% code sharing as possible. To overcome the non-shareable UI code, Xamarin.Forms was created. If you look at Figure 2-1, you can see how the solution works schematically.

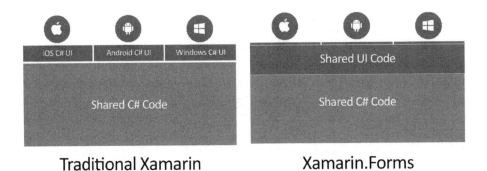

Traditional Xamarin   **Xamarin.Forms**

Figure 2-1. *Schematic view of traditional Xamarin versus Xamarin.Forms*

In the image on the left, we see the traditional approach, as it is now known with the introduction of Xamarin.Forms. The big box on the bottom is the shared C# backend code. If your application has a thought trough architecture, you would be able to share between 60% to 80% of your code across platforms. Figure 2-1 shows three platforms, but these are swappable with any other supported platform right now.

When you look on the right side of Figure 2-1, you will see a layer called the "shared UI code" . This is where the Xamarin.Forms magic is happening. According to Xamarin you would now be able to share up to 99% of your code across all platforms. While this sounds great in the marketing plans, in practice 99% cannot be achieved, unless your app is very basic.

So, how does Xamarin.Forms work? To put it simply: they added an abstraction layer on top of the UI for all platforms and transform the controls into their native counterparts for you. By using Forms, you can declare a `Button`, which is turned into a `UIButton` when running on iOS, or a `Android.Button` when running on Android. To achieve this, Xamarin implemented *platform renderers*. Each visual element on-screen has its own renderer that's responsible for converting the abstract control to the native control. I go into the workings of the renderers a bit more at the end of this chapter. An overview of all controls and everything that Xamarin. Forms offers can be found in the next chapter.

This rendering is what makes Xamarin.Forms unique, transforming controls into their native counterparts. Other solutions that offer cross-platform development will offer you a set of controls that are styled to look the same on all platforms, or maybe you can even style them using web technologies like HTML and CSS. While it might be a requirement that your app looks identical across all platforms, I think that approach of looking precisely identical on all platforms only works in very rare cases. Normally, the user will expect that the tabs in an iOS application will appear at the bottom and the tabs on Android appear on the top of the screen. With Xamarin.Forms, the controls will always look like users on any target platform would normally expect them to look—tabs will be at the bottom on iOS and on the top with Android. Xamarin.Forms takes care of making that happen automatically.

How to Construct the Layout

To define the abstract layout, Xamarin.Forms offers two ways: through XAML (eXtensible Application Markup Language) or using code. Both can be used and mixed if you want, and both have the same abilities. The choice of code or XAML comes down to taste more than anything. Yet, I see a lot of XAML being used, and I myself am a fan as well. I explain why in a little bit.

First, let's zoom in on XAML a bit more. If you have ever worked with Windows Presentation Foundation (WPF) or Universal Windows Platform (UWP) before, you might already know what XAML is and what you can do with it. The acronym looks a lot like XML, and actually XAML and XML look a lot alike when implemented. XAML makes it possible to define a layout in a XML-like design language. Listing 2-1 shows an example.

Listing 2-1. The Default Generated XAML Page in a new Xamarin.Forms Project

```
<?xml version="1.0" encoding="utf-8"?>
<ContentPage xmlns="http://xamarin.com/schemas/2014/forms"
xmlns:x="http://schemas.microsoft.com/winfx/2009/xaml"
xmlns:local="clr-namespace:Test" x:Class="Test.TestPage">
    <Label Text="Welcome to Xamarin Forms!"
VerticalOptions="Center" HorizontalOptions="Center" />
</ContentPage>
```

In Listing 2-1, you see the code that is generated for a new Xamarin. Forms project. You do not have to be a very experienced developer to see that a ContentPage is defined, and it has a Label on it. If you ran this app, you would see Xamarin.Forms at work. Figure 2-2 shows the output in the iOS simulator (left) and the Android emulator (right).

Figure 2-2. *The output of the XAML in Listing 2-1 in iOS (left) and Android (right)*

As I mentioned earlier, you might know XAML from WPF. In this Windows-oriented technology, WPF was first introduced as a replacement for WinForms. However, there are some minor differences between the two. In a matter of speaking, Xamarin has introduced another dialect. For instance, in WPF XAML you could use a `StackPanel`, whereas in Xamarin. Forms XAML, this is a `StackLayout`. Reportedly this was mainly done so the naming would feel more at home on mobile devices. Another, completely unconfirmed, theory is that it also had the advantage that developers could not just copy and paste their WPF layouts into an app and call it a day. They had to rethink their designs and adjust them to make them look and feel right on mobile devices.

Figure 2-3 shows the differences between a similar layout in Xamarin. Forms on the left and a UWP application on the right.

```
<!-- Xamarin.Forms XAML -->                         <!-- UWP XAML -->
<ContentView>                                       <UserControl>
    <StackLayout Orientation="Horizontal">              <StackPanel Orientation="Horizontal">

        <Label Text="Work Order #"                          <TextBlock Text="Work Order #"
               VerticalOptions="Center"/>                               VerticalAlignment="Center" />

        <Entry Placeholder="Enter your work order"          <TextBox PlaceholderText="Enter your work order"
               Text="{Binding WONumber, Mode=TwoWay}"/>               Text="{Binding WONumber, Mode=TwoWay}" />

        <Button Text="Save"                                 <Button Content="Save"
                TextColor="White"                                   Foreground="White"
                BackgroundColor="#77D065"                           Background="#77D065"
                Command="{Binding SaveCommand}"/>                   Command="{Binding SaveCommand}" />

    </StackLayout>                                       </StackPanel>
</ContentView>                                       </UserControl>
```

Figure 2-3. *Differences in XAML dialect between Xamarin.Forms (left) and UWP (right)*

At the Microsoft Build conference of 2017, Microsoft announced that they would start working on a XAML Standard. In an effort to unify all the dialects that are currently out there, like UWP and Xamarin, one definition will be introduced that can be used on all these platforms.

Tip   If you're interested in contributing to the XAML Standard specification, you can! It will be completely open source. At the time of writing, they are working on getting the specification right. The first draft has been published recently and you can follow it on GitHub at `https://github.com/Microsoft/xaml-standard`.

Let's go back to the question posed earlier for a moment: should you use code or XAML for your layout?

I did mention the functionality is exactly the same, so don't worry there. If you like to do it in code, I won't judge you. But I see most people doing the layout in XAML, including myself.

Writing the UI in XAML looks more structured to me, and it is more readable. Also, your view should not contain any logic. With XAML that is easier to maintain. You can't easily cheat by entering a line of code, because its only purpose is to do the layout, so you cannot use code in there. That is where the real advantage lays: it cleanly separates your UI from your code. This is especially true if you implement a pattern like Model-View-ViewModel (MVVM). You will see how this works later on when we get hands-on.

If you do it right, you can swap out another view and change not one thing in your code. You could even do that at runtime, depending on the feature toggle, if you like. The purists even like to throw away the code-behind file. When you create a XAML page, you will get `MyPage.xaml` and `MyPage.xaml.cs` files. In the latter file, you could still do all sorts of logic. But you also could get rid of it so you will not be tempted to do that. Being honest, I do like the idea, but it's not always realistic. For simple apps, it might be doable, but if you want to implement more advanced UI features, a of code in your code-behind can come in quite handy. Just make sure that it only handles UI!

Platform Renderers

To go from an abstract `Button` to the native equivalent, Xamarin.Forms uses something called a *platform renderer*. At runtime, the XAML (or code) is interpreted, and each visual element goes to its respective renderer. Combined, this will output the native layout. Of course, this will cause some overhead when loading pages, but this is mostly negligible.

Note   The performance of Forms is something that is discussed often. There is still a lot to gain there. Xamarin.Forms version 3.0 is mainly focused on implementing more performance and stability. By the time you are reading this book, this next major version of Xamarin.Forms should be out. More on this version can be found in the last part of this book.

Look at Figure 2-4 underneath to see how the translation of a Button would go.

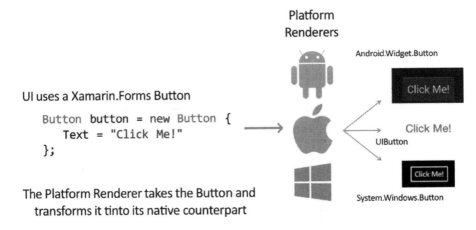

Figure 2-4. *Translation of a Button type through the platform renderer*

The great thing about this solution is, that you—as the developer—can also hook into these renderers. If you have read closely, you will have noticed how I said that each visual element goes through its respective renderer. This means, for each page, layout, and control (which you will see in the next chapter), there is a renderer available. That renderer instantiates a new control of the native kind and maps each property from the abstract Forms layout to that native control.

For instance, look at the somewhat more complex example in Figure 2-5. You can see a piece of XAML on the right and the result of that XAML on three different platforms on the left.

Figure 2-5. *More complex XAML layout on three different platforms*

Let's take out the iOS example and the Button that is in the XAML. When this button runs through the renderer, an iOS UIButton will be created. Then, the Text property will be applied by calling the UIButton.SetTitle method on iOS, because that is how you set the text for a button on iOS. Android, Windows, and any other platform have their own properties for that and thus the implementation of those renderers can and will look completely different.

With Forms, Xamarin has implemented a lot of properties and controls but not all. The visual elements they have implemented are the ones that are available on all platforms. The button, label, and textbox controls are available on all platforms, so these will be in Xamarin.Forms by default. A control that is specific to one platform will not be found in the default control set. Also, a control that is available on all platforms might have a property that is not available on all platforms. There is a good chance that this also isn't implemented in Xamarin.Forms. However, this does not mean that you cannot use it!

Today, there are several ways to use these platform-specific options nonetheless. The most obvious one, but not necessarily the best one, is to use a *custom renderer*. We will see how this works in practice later on in this book, but I will give you a quick preview right now. To make some specific controls or properties of controls available, you can inherit from the renderers already in place. That way, you can override the behavior that Xamarin has provided for you with your own behaviors.

As another way to customize just a few properties on a control, Xamarin introduced the so-called *Effects*. You can think of these Effects as lightweight custom renderers. Using Xamarin Effects is preferred for smaller styling changes, as they impact the performance less than custom renderer do.

The last feature that was introduced in Xamarin.Forms is called *native embedding*. With native embedding, Forms enables you to reference actual native controls from shared code or XAML. This means that you can mix the abstract UI code with native components from the platform you are targeting. The native controls will then only be rendered only on the platform that your app runs on at that time. This means that you can have a page that includes a `Xamarin.Forms.Button`, an iOS `UILabel`, and a Android `RatingBar`. On iOS, you will see the button and the label; on Android, you will see the button and the rating control.

Note   Not all of these methods will be handled in this book. If you want to read more on this particular subject, look at the Xamarin documentation. For Effects, look at `https://developer.xamarin.com/guides/xamarin-forms/application-fundamentals/effects/` and for native embedding, see the page at `https://developer.xamarin.com/guides/xamarin-forms/user-interface/layouts/add-platform-controls/`.

Summary

This chapter explained what Xamarin.Forms is from a high-level overview. You learned that it is a very powerful addition to Xamarin and that it can help you push your code-sharing percentage to the max. Furthermore, you learned that you can use Forms either through code or by using XAML and what the benefits and drawbacks of those choices are.

Finally, the chapter went a little more in-depth on how Xamarin. Forms achieves the translation to native controls by looking into platform renderers and how they work.

The next chapter covers what is contained in the Xamarin.Forms package. It describes the different pages, layouts, and controls more extensively.

CHAPTER 3

Xamarin.Forms Contents

Let's take a closer look at what Xamarin.Forms has to offer. In the previous chapter, you learned that the main problem that Forms tries to solve is the need for separate UI code on each platform. To do this, Xamarin introduced an abstraction layer with which you can define the UI for all platforms. This abstraction layer is nothing more than a NuGet package with a set of libraries.

I want to emphasize the abstraction layer, because I sometimes hear that people claim to have built a Xamarin.Forms app. Although that seems like a perfectly normal way to communicate that you used Xamarin. Forms in your app, there is no such thing as a "Xamarin.Forms app". When compiled, it will still produce one app per platform. If you are targeting iOS and Android, you will still end up with `.ipa` and `.apk` files—the equivalent of an `.exe` file on a desktop—and they will still be two native apps. Xamarin.Forms is just a tool that can make the development process easier. With that misunderstanding out of the way, let's look at what Xamarin.Forms has to offer in a more technical sense.

© Gerald Versluis 2017
G. Versluis, *Xamarin.Forms Essentials*, https://doi.org/10.1007/978-1-4842-3240-8_3

Portable Class Library vs Shared Project

The first thing that is good to know is that there are two ways to set up a Xamarin.Forms application. You can use a Portable Class Library (PCL) or a shared project.

There are a lot of (heated) discussions on the Internet about the one being better than the other. I believe it mostly comes down to a matter of taste. Let me walk you through the differences.

The main difference is that a PCL will result in a separate binary DLL file, while a shared project will be compiled into your app. That being said, I'm just going to come out and say I'm a PCL-ist. I just like the thought that my shared code is physically separated from the rest of the program. Figure 3-1 shows a schematic overview of how a PCL compiles into binaries. You see how the respective apps reference the binary that the PCL project produces.

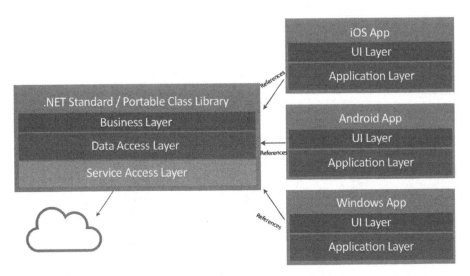

Figure 3-1. *Schematic of the use of a PCL or .NET Standard library*

There is one big downside to the PCL, which is not such a downside anymore. The way a PCL works is that it supports only the .NET Framework subset of all targeted platforms. In the properties of your PCL, you can specify which platforms you are targeting. Say you have .NET Framework 4.5, Xamarin.iOS, and Xamarin.Android. If a piece of functionality *is* available in all three, it is supported in your PCL. If some method or class is *not* supported on Xamarin.iOS, but *is* supported on .NET Framework 4.5 and Xamarin.Android, the method or class is *not* supported in your PCL.

All these subset variants are linked to PCL profiles. These profiles are identified with three digits, such as 259 or 111. Each profile stands for a combination of targeted platforms, 259 and 111 being the most common in Xamarin.

In the beginning, the NuGet packages weren't prepared for this. So, when you tried to install one on your PCL, chances were that your profile wasn't supported and you could not use the NuGet package. But by now most of the NuGet packages that you would want to use support the common PCL profiles used by Xamarin apps.

A shared project is literally that. It's a folder with files that contain source code and, depending on which platform you are building at that time, the code is taken from that shared folder and included in the app. Figure 3-2 shows how the code on the left also contains all platform-specific code and is *compiled in the app,* instead of referencing it.

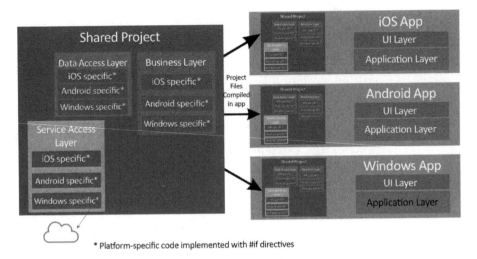

Figure 3-2. *Schematic of the use of a shared project*

Near the end of this chapter I will tell you about the
DependencyService, which enables you to access platform-specific
features from your shared code. The way that you access platform-specific
features in a shared project is by using compiler directives. You know,
pieces of code like this:

```
#if __ANDROID__
```

In my humble opinion, this litters your code and makes it unreadable
at best. When using a PCL, you can stick the cross-platform code in its own
project instead of using everything together. More on that later.

In this book, I use a PCL project, but of course you are free to use a
shared project at will. To read more extensively on the differences, as well
as the pros and cons, visit the documentation page at https://developer.
xamarin.com/guides/cross-platform/application_fundamentals/
code-sharing/.

The .NET Standard

There is another player in the PCL/shared project discussion that I didn't mention yet: the .NET Standard library. The use of .NET Standard libraries in Xamarin apps will be the future. With the .NET Standard specification implemented, you will have a true cross-platform library that can be used on iOS, Android, Linux, your Xbox, and whatever platform will support the .NET Standard in the future.

The working would be very similar to the use of PCLs right now, only not based on profiles, but on the .NET Standard version. At the time of writing, there is support for .NET Standard on Xamarin, but it isn't the default yet. Also, it kind of has the same startup problems the PCL had, if a NuGet you want to use does not support your preferred .NET Standard version yet, you can't use it in your project until they do start supporting it.

In this book, when we start looking at the example application, I will be using a PCL for the shared code. Simply because at the time of writing, not all NuGets were updated for the use of .NET Standard. However, turning your PCL into a .NET Standard library in the (near) future should not be too hard. There are already some resources on this out there, like this very nice one at `https://xamarinhelp.com/upgrade-pcl-net-standard-class-library/`.

Just before the release of this book, the .NET Standard templates for Visual Studio were released. As of Visual Studio 2017 version 15.5 the PCL will be phased out in favor of the .NET Standard library. Projects build with a PCL today will still be supported though. For more information have a look at this blog post: *https://blog.xamarin.com/net-standard-comes-xamarin-forms-project-templates/*.

Pages, Layouts, and Controls

At the time of writing, Forms provides you with:

- Five types of pages
- Seven types of layouts
- Twenty-four controls

Figure 3-3 shows an overview of the pages and layouts with their schematic representation.

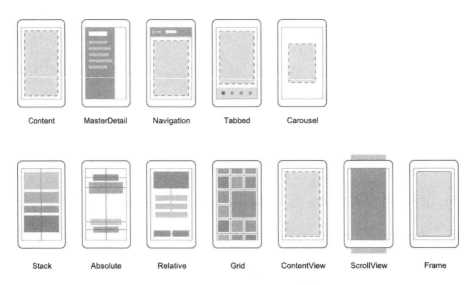

Figure 3-3. *All the pages and layouts available in Xamarin.Forms*

Before I describe them all to you in a bit more detail, it is good to know how pages and layouts work together. The contents of a page can consist of only one child layout. However, layouts can be nested. This way, virtually any type of layout can be achieved. You place controls in a layout.

Note how I say "the contents of a page". As you will see in a minute, some pages take other pages as children, but only one page is shown at a time. For instance, a TabbedPage contains a collection of other pages, but shows only one at a time. The page shown in a tab will have to contain a layout.

Here's a quick description of the page types:

- **ContentPage**: An empty container that you can fill any way you like. It does not have any specific layout by itself.

- **MasterDetailPage**: Probably best known for its notorious "hamburger menu". By the use of a button or swiping the screen from left to right, a menu page will appear, and this is the *master* part of the page. On the right side, the *detail* part of the page is shown. Whenever the user chooses some option on the master page, they will drill down into that and details of that option will be shown in the detail view. Both the master and the detail are just a ContentPage for you to design.

- **NavigationPage**: Provides you with a basic navigation stack. Whenever you push a page on the stack, it will be on top. When you press the Back button—either the one on the top bar in the screen or the physical one on the device—the page is removed and the previous page is shown.

- **TabbedPage**: Lets you divide the screen with tabs. Each tab has its own type of page, which can be any of the other pages, basically. Not all pages work together nicely out of the box.

- **CarouselPage**: Used to add multiple pages so the user can swipe through them to the right or left. Note that the CarouselPage will be deprecated in a future release. There will be a successor, the CarouselView, which is available in a separate NuGet package at the time of writing. If you want to use this functionality, use CarouselView.

The layouts are grouped together. I describe only the ones I use the most.

- **StackLayout**: Stacks all child controls either vertically (default) or horizontally. Note that a `StackLayout` will only take as much space as needed. If the child controls combined are only 100x100, the `StackLayout` will only be 100x100. This can sometimes cause a control not to show up when wrapped in a `StackLayout`.

- **Grid**: Used to build a more advanced layout with columns and rows. You'll probably find yourself using this a lot, as well as `StackLayout`.

- **ScrollView**: When you suspect your content might grow out of view, wrap it in a `ScrollView`. The OS will detect if the user can't reach all of the elements and make all its children scrollable. Note that some controls—like the `ListView`—already have scrolling abilities. Do not wrap these controls in a `ScrollView`, because unexpected behavior might occur.

- **AbsoluteLayout and RelativeLayout**: These layouts are for more advanced scenarios. In short, the `AbsoluteLayout` is used to arrange views by coordinates and sizes in absolute values or ratios. The `RelativeLayout` is used for setting constraints relative to their parents' size and location. These layouts will not be handled in this book. To read more about them, refer to the documentation at `https://developer.xamarin.com/guides/xamarin-forms/user-interface/layouts/`.

- **ContentView**: This is basically the base class for a new layout you might want to create yourself.

- **Frame**: Can contain a single element. Of course, nesting can be used and can provide some framing options like showing a border and a drop shadow.

Tip   When you start building more complex layouts over time, I highly recommend getting a better understanding of how they work. It is very easy to mess up the performance of your app by using layouts incorrectly. Dos and don'ts on applying a layout can be found in a session on Evolve 2016 by Jason Smith, lead engineer of Xamarin.Forms. Kent Boogaart has been so kind to put it into writing at `http://kent-boogaart.com/blog/jason-smith%27s-xamarin-forms-performance-tips`. A recording of the session can be found on YouTube at `https://www.youtube.com/watch?v=RZvdql3EvOE`.

Of all these layouts, you will probably use StackLayout and Grid the most. Also, these will be the ones most often used in this book. Keep in mind these few most important rules regarding Grid and StackLayout. Memorize these rules from the start:

- Do *not* use a StackLayout to host a single child.

- Do *not* use a Grid when a StackLayout suffices.

- Do *not* use multiple StackLayouts when a Grid suffices.

- *Do* use star-sized grid columns/rows rather than auto-sized ones.

- Do *not* use multiple StackLayouts to simulate a Grid.

- *Do* use a Grid to achieve layering.

I won't describe all the controls in detail, but you will see some of them along the way, mainly in Chapter 6 when you start building screens. For now, it is enough to know that the most basic controls, like input fields, toggles, date pickers, etc., are all there. Figure 3-4 is an overview of all the controls that are packaged with Xamarin.Forms by default.

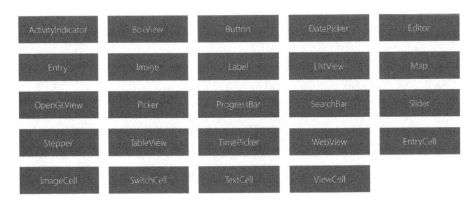

Figure 3-4. *Controls that come with Xamarin.Forms*

In the future, more controls might be added. There are also some good vendors out there, such as like Telerik, SyncFusion, DevExpress, and ComponentOne. These parties have mainly paid controls, but there is also a lot available through open source.

If you look closely at Figure 3-4, note that the last five controls all end with `Cell`. These controls can only be used in a `ListView` or `TableView`. You will see how to use some of them later.

When you dig deeper into Xamarin.Forms you might find that a fairly basic control isn't in the default set or a trivial property is missing. For instance, you might expect that an `Entry` would have a property to constrain the maximum length that is entered. There is no property for that; you have to implement one. Although many features are available in the form of NuGet packages and example code, don't be surprised if something you need isn't supported (yet).

Personally, I think this is due to the fact that Xamarin.Forms is relatively young and went through a lot in a small period of time. The initial focus was to get everything stable and performant, and maybe after that we will see some more default functionalities in the controls.

If you're brave enough, of course, you could just open the the Xamarin. Forms source code, as it is now open source, implement something entirely new, and then open up a pull request. Even if you're not quite that brave yet, it might be refreshing sometimes to see what is going on in the internals. If you are interested, look at `https://github.com/xamarin/Xamarin.Forms`.

But There Is More…

Besides all the visual-related goodies that come with Xamarin.Forms, there is more.

Most importantly, it has everything to support the MVVM pattern out of the box. It has support for two-way data binding and has something called the `DependencyService` on-board to accommodate dependency injection.

DependencyService

`DependencyService` has another very important task in the Xamarin.Forms ecosystem: reaching native code while sharing as much code as possible. That sounds a bit cryptic, right? Let's take a little step back first.

The team behind Xamarin.Forms implemented the most important features to be able to achieve maximum code sharing. But there will *always* be scenarios where code sharing is simply not possible. For instance, think of the fingerprint scanners on phones. I believe Apple brought the fingerprint scanner to the big audience with success for the first time. While some other devices had the capability, there were only few and it didn't have much support in the OS.

At that time, when you wanted to support the use of the fingerprint reader in your app, you had to use platform-specific code. Even now that other vendors have adopted the fingerprint readers, you still need to write platform-specific code, because the APIs are totally different and Xamarin. Forms does not offer a unified API for it. In this specific case—and probably many other cases—there are plugins available for it. But still it's good to know how you can reach platform-specific code if need be. This is where DependencyService comes in.

Another example that is often used in this context is Text-To-Speech (TTS). To enable TTS in your app and still share a maximum amount of code, you define an interface with the methods that you want to use in your app. Look at Listing 3-1 for example.

Listing 3-1. The Interface for Our TTS Implementation

```
public interface ITextToSpeech
{
    void Speak (string text);
}
```

This is a very simple interface, which just states that one method should be implemented, namely Speak. This method will receive a string, and the text in that string will be spoken out loud by the platform's TTS engine.

Note   For a class to work with the DependencyService, it must have a parameterless constructor.

This interface should be defined in your shared code, in my case the PCL project. To reach platform-specific code, we would want to implement this interface on the targeted platform. For this example, let's use the iOS project. Create a new class there, which implements the ITextToSpeech interface. In Listing 3-2, you can see how to do that. Note that the actual code might be deprecated, but that is irrelevant for now.

Listing 3-2. Implementation of the ITextToSpeech Interface on iOS

```
using AVFoundation;
using DependencyServiceSample.iOS;

[assembly: Xamarin.Forms.Dependency (typeof
(TextToSpeechImplementation))]
public class TextToSpeechImplementation : ITextToSpeech
{
    public TextToSpeechImplementation () {}

    public void Speak (string text)
    {
        var speechSynthesizer = new AVSpeechSynthesizer ();

        var speechUtterance = new AVSpeechUtterance (text) {
            Rate = AVSpeechUtterance.MaximumSpeechRate/4,
            Voice = AVSpeechSynthesisVoice.FromLanguage
            ("en-US"),
            Volume = 0.5f,
            PitchMultiplier = 1.0f
        };

        speechSynthesizer.SpeakUtterance (speechUtterance);
    }
}
```

While it is still C# code, you suddenly see some iOS specific namespaces and types. For the TTS to work on iOS, we need to work with the AVSpeechSynthesizer. This type is not available to us in shared code nor on Android or any other platform, but we can use it on iOS.

The main piece of code to take note of here is the assembly attribute above the class. With this attribute, we register this class as a dependency to the DependencyService at runtime.

If we go back to the shared code, to some place where we would want to call the code to speak our text out loud, we can simply call this line of code:

```
DependencyService.Get<ITextToSpeech>().Speak("Hello from
Xamarin Forms");
```

You can call upon the DependencyService's Get method to retrieve the implementation of the interface that you provide, in our case the ITextToSpeech, and it will give you the class for the platform you are using. With this very powerful piece of tooling, you can go back and forth between platform-specific and shared code. And as long as you stick to interchangeable types, return values are supported as well.

In real life, be sure to check if the outcome of the Get method is not null. If for some reason the registration of the dependency did not take, or you forgot the attribute above the class, it will return null.

The implementation of Android will mostly be the same, except for the code that is in the body of the Speak method. There will be some code that is specific to Android and will look suspiciously like Java. We will see more examples of this in the example application later on.

Navigation

Furthermore, Xamarin.Forms holds a helper class for navigating between pages. By calling the INavigation implementation on any VisualElement, you can navigate around easily. The navigation helper is contextual, which means that it will choose the right way of navigating between two pages.

You will see later on, when I talk more about implementing the MVVM pattern, that I don't use the built-in navigation capabilities of Xamarin. Forms. It's good to know it's there when you need it!

Animations API

To help you create slick applications, Xamarin.Forms includes an animations API. This abstract layer over the platform's native animation capabilities helps you add great-looking animations, without having to write platform-specific code for it. The most elemental effects are implemented for you to use. I'm not much of an animator myself, so I don't use this API very often. There is a great plugin called Lottie that can help you implement some eye candy. More on that later.

Messaging Center

Last but not least, there is the Messaging Center. If you cannot find another way to reach another class without hard referencing it, the message bus is at your disposal. With the Messaging Center, you can send a notification across your app when some event occurs. Listeners can then execute code whenever a specific message is fired. Although I believe that this should be used as a last resort, there are definitely use cases for this method.

Since I will not be describing it extensively in the rest of this book, let's look at a short example now.

The Messaging Center is made up of two parts: *send* and *subscribe*. To send a message on the bus, you can simply use `MessagingCenter. Send<MainPage> (this, "Hi");`.

This sends a message with the recipient being of the type `MainPage` and the sender being `this`, which will be the instance of `MainPage` at that time. The message being sent is always a string, in this case `"Hi"`. There are some overloads for this that allow you to send values as arguments.

To subscribe to this same message at another place in your application, you can use the code in Listing 3-3.

Listing 3-3. Subscribing to a Message Using the Messaging Center

```
MessagingCenter.Subscribe<MainPage> (this, "Hi", (sender) => {
    // do something whenever the "Hi" message is sent
});
```

The important part here is that you subscribe to the message that has the `MainPage` type as a recipient. Of course, this can be any type; `MainPage` is just an example. This, in conjunction with the message identifier (`"Hi"`), will subscribe to that specific message.

Again, I like to stay clear of using this as much as I can, but sometimes it can be useful. One specific case is when you use a `MasterDetailPage` in your app and you navigate to a certain page but do not use the main menu. I still want the main menu to reflect that the user is now in another part of the app by highlighting the menu item the user lands in. In this case, I send a message on the message bus and subscribe from the menu page. I do not want to create all kinds of references to achieve a simple UI effect.

To read more on the use of the Messaging Center, you can turn to the Xamarin documentation page at `https://developer.xamarin.com/ guides/xamarin-forms/application-fundamentals/messaging-center/`.

Summary

I hope I have been able to give you a complete overview of what is included in the Xamarin.Forms package. It is a lot to take in and maybe it won't stick all at once. Don't worry about it now. When you start working hands-on with the sample app in Chapter 5, things will probably start to fall into place.

This chapter covered the elements that come with Xamarin.Forms and are there for you to use to design your screens. Besides that, we looked at other tools that are included, like navigation and the animation API. I explained the difference between using a PCL project and shared project as a code sharing strategy and how to write platform-specific code when using a PCL through the DependencyService. To top it off, you saw a small example of the Messaging Center. It decoupled the code using a message bus that is built-in with Forms.

The next chapter discusses when to use Xamarin.Forms versus when to use traditional Xamarin.

CHAPTER 4

Xamarin.Forms vs. Traditional Xamarin

In the previous chapters, I talked about what Xamarin.Forms is and where it fits within the existing Xamarin technology. Xamarin.Forms was never intended to replace the Xamarin technology as a whole. Forms is merely offering another alternative to maximize code sharing by making it possible to define the UI in a unified way.

Soon after the introduction of Xamarin.Forms, the original approach of building apps with Xamarin was renamed "traditional Xamarin". This chapter explains when to choose which approach and what you have to keep in mind when you do.

What Is Traditional Xamarin?

The answer to this question might already be apparent to you from reading the previous chapters, but I want to describe it in more detail. Initially, Xamarin offers a way for developers to create cross-platform applications backed by the .NET technologies and all the wonderful things that come with it. By the means of the C# language, people can reach out to users with all kinds of devices.

© Gerald Versluis 2017
G. Versluis, *Xamarin.Forms Essentials*, https://doi.org/10.1007/978-1-4842-3240-8_4

Way back when I started my career, mobile development piqued my interest. From my study, I had some experience with a variety of languages, but C# stuck and I knew that was where I wanted to go. At that time, there was little choice and I started looking into the world of Windows Phone development. However, I had an iPhone and am still very fond of them to this day.

At some point, I got word of a program that allowed you to receive a phone, the infamous Nokia Lumia 800, on which you could develop and test. If you successfully published three apps to the store by a certain date, the phone would be yours. All you had to do was pitch these three apps to Microsoft. And so, I did. I came up with three apps, which were approved, got the phone, and started developing. It was great! I had a good time, but the Windows Phone just wasn't for me. The development was a breeze, though, and I could create applications that ran on a phone with the tools and language that I know and love.

After a little while I decided to give iOS development a try. I bought an iMac and opened Xcode; I was scared! Of course, I did look into Objective-C. I figured if thousands of people could do it, so could I. But the Xcode IDE is much different than the Microsoft .NET ecosystem. I did give it a go, but it never took off.

A similar thing happened with Android, but the tools were more alike and I had some experience with Java. The tooling and Android as an OS just doesn't really cut it for me. Besides, I just didn't have the time or resources to master two more languages and the accompanying tools.

In the meantime, I visited some conferences and learned that MonoTouch was transforming into Xamarin. I started looking into this interesting company and their techniques and now, here I am, writing another book on the subject.

The point of all this is that I believe Xamarin has made cross-platform development accessible to a lot more people. If they had not made it possible to create apps with C#, a lot of people would probably never have gotten into mobile development.

But back to traditional Xamarin. Xamarin basically created a lot of wrappers around the native APIs and is maintaining them. That means that you are still using a lot of Java and Objective-C kind of types, but by the means of C#, including all the great features that C# offers and with the rich IDE that Visual Studio offers. There is still a learning curve for picking up some platform-specific methodologies, but Xamarin has taken away most of the pain.

The only thing that was standing in the way of sharing most of your code was the user interface. Apple has multiple options for iOS, but the common way to design the UI is by using storyboards. In Figure 4-1, you can see the storyboard designer.

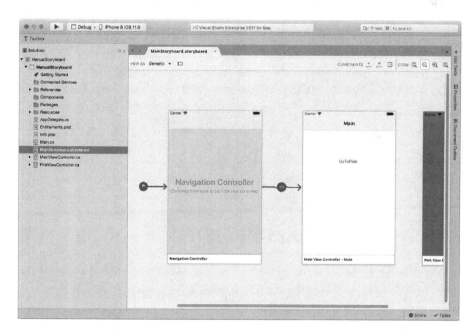

Figure 4-1. *iOS storyboard designer showing some screens and the flow between them*

To facilitate the development process, Xamarin made the Xcode storyboard designer available from the plugin in Visual Studio for Windows and Mac. That way, you still have the power and ease that Apple put into the designer, but you won't have to leave the safety of Visual Studio.

The same goes for Android. Actually, designing screens on Android is similar to XAML in Xamarin.Forms. Google also implemented the building of screens by using XML. Note that on Android these files have the default `.xml` extension, whereas on Xamarin.Android you will need to use the `.axml` extension. An Android designer is available as well; it's included in Visual Studio by Xamarin, just like the iOS one.

Since this book focuses on the use of Xamarin.Forms, I won't go into the Xamarin.iOS and Xamarin.Android designers. To read more on these, refer to the respective Xamarin documentation pages at `https://developer.xamarin.com/guides/ios/user_interface/designer/` and `https://developer.xamarin.com/guides/android/user_interface/android-designer/`.

Knowing all this, the main difference between traditional Xamarin and Xamarin.Forms is the fact that the UI code isn't shared among the different platform projects.

Which One Do You Choose?

Xamarin has an official statement on when to choose traditional Xamarin and when to choose Xamarin.Forms. Figure 4-2 shows this statement.

Figure 4-2. *When to choose traditional and when to choose Forms according to the Xamarin web site*

When you value code sharing over platform-specific features, you should choose Forms. The vice versa is true as well. Moreover, Xamarin specifically talks about choosing a custom UI over code sharing.

This opinion that Forms is valuable only when code sharing is important seems to be shared by a fair amount of people. Xamarin.Forms would not be fit with polished user interfaces. Therefore, apps built with Xamarin.Forms could never be truly popular.

Personally, I think the claim that Forms is not ideal for creating polished interfaces is only partly true. I think the issue is more one of mindset. Sure, when working with traditional Xamarin applications, it will probably be a bit easier to create polished interfaces for each platform. Creating custom tailored user interfaces with native tools will probably feel more intuitive. But this will automatically mean that no code sharing will happen at this point.

What is definitely *not* true is that by using Xamarin.Forms, you will not have full access to every API needed to create a great user interface. Remember, Xamarin.Forms is only a helper that provides you with an abstraction layer to define the UI in a shareable manner. If you want to divert from this, you can!

Using Custom Renderers

You can use custom renderers to override the implementation that Xamarin provides and write your own implementation in a custom renderer. You will see how to use this in practice later on, but let me fill you in on the basics here.

As you might remember, each on-screen visual element has its own renderer. The renderer will take in the abstract Xamarin.Forms control and instantiate the native control for you, mapping the properties that you specified. Figure 4-3 illustrates this concept using the Entry control.

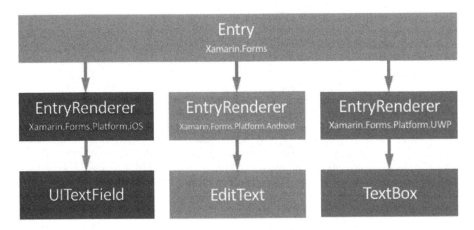

Figure 4-3. *How the Entry control is rendered into its native counterpart*

If you're not completely satisfied with the way the control looks after it goes through the renderer, you can hook into it and customize it. Creating a custom renderer is actually pretty easy. Let's stick with the Entry control as an example. If you wanted to change anything about the border of the input field, you have to use a custom renderer, as the Xamarin.Forms APIs don't account for this.

To do this, you create a new class in the platform project that you want to customize the control for. Remember, you only have access to native code—and thus to native properties and methods—from within the platform project. Listing 4-1 shows a sample implementation of the custom renderer in the iOS project.

Listing 4-1. Implementation of the Custom Renderer for the Entry Control on iOS

```
using Xamarin.Forms.Platform.iOS;
using CustomRendererSample.iOS;
using Xamarin.Forms;

[assembly: ExportRenderer (typeof(Entry),
typeof(CustomEntryRenderer))]
namespace CustomRendererSample.iOS
{
    public class CustomEntryRenderer : EntryRenderer
    {
        protected override void OnElementChanged
        (ElementChangedEventArgs<Entry> e)
        {
            base.OnElementChanged (e);

            if (Control != null)
            {
```

```
                    // do whatever you want to the UITextField
                    here!
                    Control.BorderStyle = UITextBorderStyle.None;
                }
            }
        }
    }
```

Let me point out the things to notice here, from top to bottom. First, look at the assembly attribute. You might remember this one from the DependencyService. You might think of a custom renderer as a dependency service for visual changes. This attribute is very important. With the assembly attribute, you specify the control that this renderer targets and the renderer that has to handle the rendering. In this case, the Entry control has to be rendered by the CustomEntryRenderer class. If you forget this, the default Xamarin.Forms renderer will be used.

The next thing to notice is that the CustomEntryRenderer inherits from the EntryRenderer class, which is the one Xamarin has implemented for us. Since we inherit the original class, we do not need to reimplement the whole rendering process again. We can just overwrite the parts that we want.

Lastly, look at the OnElementChanged method and its implementation. This is usually the method you want to override whenever you are making changes to a control. The first thing you want to do is call the base method, so Xamarin.Forms will do all the default rendering, and after that you can add your own customizations. Then there is a check if the Control property is not null, and if not, the border is set to none.

The Xamarin.Forms control, in this case the Entry, is provided through the method's argument. The Control property of the render class holds the native control.

And that's it! This is all that is needed to create a custom renderer for all the Entry controls in your application. However, there will likely be situations where you do not want to override the renderer on all controls of one type. Because of that, it is pretty common to create an inheritance of the control that you want to customize first. If we would have created a custom control named MyEntry first and named the renderer MyEntryRenderer, the result (when implementing custom renderers for each platform) would look like Figure 4-4.

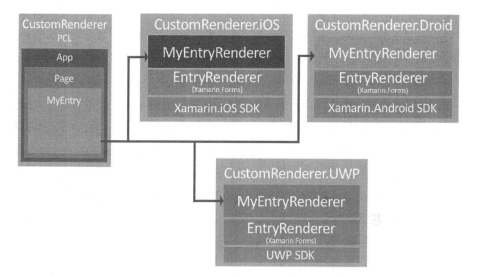

Figure 4-4. *Overview of the implementation of custom renderers on all platforms*

You don't have to implement a custom renderer on all platforms. If you want to adjust something on iOS, but not on Android, you can implement the renderer on the one and not the other. The default renderer will then be used on the Android platform.

Recall that custom renderers are not always needed. There are other more lightweight solutions, like using an Effect, which is recommended for minor UI tweaks.

Tip There is some misconception in the community about the "no custom UI with Xamarin.Forms" statement. For example, Steven Thewissen and Adam Pedley have written blog posts in which they try to prove this statement wrong. They try to do this by recreating the user interfaces of popular apps in the store. Look at this link for a recreation of Twitter: `https://www.thewissen.io/xamarin-forms-ui-twitter/`. Or take a look at Runkeeper at `https://www.thewissen.io/xamarin-forms-ui-runkeeper/` and finally, Instagram, at `https://xamarinhelp.com/creating-instagram-ui-xamarin-forms/`. All of this goodness is built in pure Xamarin.Forms.

Summary

Choosing traditional Xamarin versus Xamarin.Forms is dependent on your requirements, previous experience, and taste. I like to think that you can always start with Xamarin.Forms as a base and, whenever you need some more customizations in your UI, you can implement custom renderers or effects. That way, you still have at least some shared code. The implementation with custom renderers, however, does adversely impact the performance, because there has to be a translation from one control to another at some point. Also, customization through a separate renderer might be considered more complicated than doing it directly on the native UI elements.

This chapter explained what traditional Xamarin is all about and how it relates to Xamarin.Forms. Most importantly, it showed you how you can still achieve customization in your user interfaces when using Xamarin.Forms.

This concludes the first part of this book. The first part was mainly about explaining what Xamarin is as a company and a technology. I tried to mix some storytelling with the technical details, so that you would be entertained and be prepared for going hands-on in the next part of this book.

The next part of the book starts looking at an actual app that is built with the help of Xamarin.Forms. By describing how I worked on this app and how certain things were implemented, I hope you will get a better understanding of how to build a Xamarin.Forms app yourself.

PART II

Building an App

CHAPTER 5

Establishing the Architecture

The first part of this book is all about the concepts of Xamarin.Forms. In this second part, we will look how Xamarin.Forms is used in an actual app that is in the store and has thousands of downloads. The app I will be using is the "been pwned" app and is available for iOS and Android. This chapter starts by telling you about the app, and then we will venture into its inner workings.

Before we can do anything, we need to establish the architecture. I will share how I like to set up a Xamarin.Forms app with the use of MVVM and how I structure the different projects.

The "Been Pwned" App

This app and I have a bit of history. Back in the day, when I was just getting started on Xamarin.Forms, I wanted to build some apps to practice my skills. The best way to do this, for me, is to have some kind of purpose. I can't just start building some dummy application that will probably never be used. I lose interest pretty fast and never finish it.

I decided to find some interesting third-party systems from which I would get my data and functionality, so I didn't have to develop the whole backend as well, because I already knew how to do that. At that time I did build some (very) simple apps, such as Instant Rimshot

(iOS: `https://itunes.apple.com/nl/app/instant-rimshot/`
`id1021902720` and Android: `https://play.google.com/store/apps/`
`details?id=com.versluisit.InstantRimshot`) and some others that
didn't make it into the store. After that I went on to build some more
serious apps. One of them was for a Dutch web site that indexes game
prices; it's called BudgetGaming (only for iOS: `https://itunes.apple.`
`com/nl/app/gamescanner/id484947088`) and is still available in the store
today with a good number of active users.

The other app I created at that time was the "Been Pwned" app. It uses
the API as made available by security expert Troy Hunt on his web site at
`https://haveibeenpwned.com/`. With this web site, Troy Hunt makes a great
effort to index databases that have been part of a hack. Whenever a web site
has been breached and data was stolen, he tries to obtain this data, verify
its authenticity, strip all the privacy-sensitive details, and make it available
through the "Have I been pwned" web site so that you can see if your details
were leaked. At this point, almost five billion accounts are in the system.

Upon discovering that the "Have I been pwned" web site also had an
API, I wanted to make an app out of it. There were a couple of apps already
out there that sourced this data, but they didn't quite cut it for me. I wanted
to make a great looking app, offering as much of the functionality similar
to the web site as possible, and be able to implement features that I didn't
use before. Actually, this was the very first project that I implemented
push notifications for. And besides all these technical reasons for wanting
to do this app, I also thought it would be awesome to contribute to the
awareness that security should be taken serious.

Now, a few years later, the initial app has been downloaded over 15,000
times between iOS and Android. Although it does what it should, the app
could use a refresh. In addition, throughout the years I have had a couple
of people who didn't trust the app. They were afraid that leaving their
data in my app would be a scam itself. I can't blame them! It would be the
perfect thing to do; pose to be fighting the good fight, but letting people
run into a trap.

To take the objections of these people away—although I understand that there will always be people who remain skeptical—I also decided to open source the code. On the one hand to show that I have nothing to hide, and on the other so people can contribute and make the app even better. And just maybe someone might learn a thing or two from how we built it.

That is also where this book comes in. I think the "been pwned" app is just about the right size to demonstrate the most essential parts of a Xamarin.Forms app that communicate with a REST backend. By writing up the process that I go through when setting up a fairly small application, I hope you will learn to do it yourself. This doesn't mean that my way is the right way, far from it. If you ask 100 developers, you'll get 102 different answers on the right way to do this. So, this is just one way that I like to do it.

This application is built with Xamarin.Forms. It uses some custom renderers and has some interesting NuGet packages and more. All things that are not very uncommon for even a relatively small app. In the next chapters, I walk you through the different parts.

All the source code for this application can be found on `https://github.com/jfversluis/been-pwned`. Although it could be that the actual source might differ at some points because of the continuous development on it. By the time you are reading this, the new version should also be in the app stores.

Another thing that might be good to know—for this book, I will be using Visual Studio for Mac. But everything that is described in this book, you can also do on Windows and Visual Studio on Windows. The actual code and solution are interchangeable between Windows and Mac. The process to get things done might be slightly different at some points, but the result will be the same. Also, there might be a slight focus on iOS since we want to release that version first.

Setting Up the Project Structure

To set up a new Xamarin.Forms app, all you have to do is click the New Project button. There is a slight difference here between Visual Studio (VS) on Windows and on Mac, but again, the result will be the same. In the dialog that comes up, there are all kinds of projects that you could start. You can see the dialog in VS for Mac in Figure 5-1.

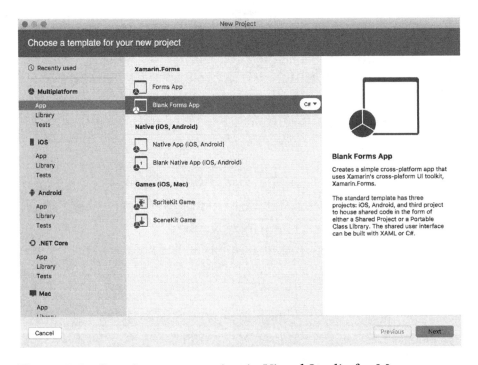

Figure 5-1. *Creating a new project in Visual Studio for Mac*

Since we are focused on Xamarin.Forms, we go into the Multiplatform section and have to make a choice between a Forms App or Blank Forms App. As the name states, the one is "more blank" than the other. If you choose the regular Forms App, you have the option to create an ASP.NET backend as well. Whether you create the backend project or not, you are still presented with some example code in your app. This can be very helpful if you are getting started for the first time, but I'm not really a big fan of code being generated for me at this point.

The Blank Forms app is just that. It creates three projects for you. The Xamarin.Forms package is installed and the rest is totally up to you.

Note   In Visual Studio for Mac, you will not be presented with the UWP project when you start a Xamarin.Forms app, simply because it is not supported (yet?). If you want to support all platforms, you will have to work from Windows, with a Mac build agent for the iOS project.

After choosing the right template, click Next. There will be some additional configuration options. The main thing you need to configure is the name of your app. The Organization Identifier is the unique identifier of your application in the stores. This identifier will look like a reversed domain name. Other things you can configure are the platform projects that are generated and whether you want to create a local Git repository for the new solution.

Been Pwned Structure

Now we skip ahead a little bit in time and look at how I structured the "been pwned" project. This isn't something that I strictly do beforehand. I like to use more of the "evolve as we go" approach, but for the order of this book, it makes sense to start describing this here. Figure 5-2 shows the build-up of this solution. For the layout of this book, I put the different projects next to each other.

As shown in Figure 5-2, there is one solution at the top level, called BeenPwned.App. Underneath that, there are three projects: BeenPwned.App. Core, BeenPwned.App.iOS, and BeenPwned.App.Droid. The Core project is the PCL, which contains all of our shared logic. The iOS and Droid projects are the bootstrap projects for each respective platform.

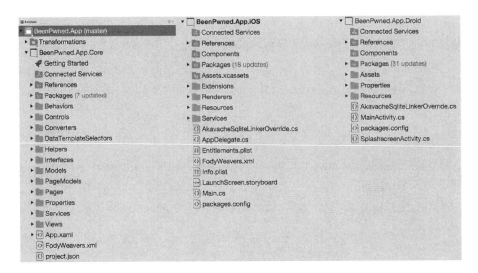

Figure 5-2. *The project structure of the been pwned app*

Tip   You might want to avoid having folders that end with .App on
a Mac. The .app extension is an executable application on MacOS
and naming a folder like this means MacOS sees it as an application
archive. While this has no implications on the working of your code
from Visual Studio, it looks a bit funny on the file system. If you do
find yourself caught in this situation and need access to the folder,
just right-click the folder and choose Show Contents.

Under each platform, you see a number of folders. If the app grows
bigger or you have a backend with which you wanted to share the models
for instance, you could move some of the code in these folders to their own
projects. Since this app does not need to share any code, I took the "Keep
It Simple Stupid" approach and just left all the code in the PCL project,
structured in folders.

You might see some folders that are named similar to some Xamarin. Forms concepts I already mentioned. I will give you a brief overview of all the folders with their contents and where you will learn more about them. In the shared project, there are these folders:

- **Behaviors**: This is where the Xamarin.Forms behaviors reside. You will learn more about this in Chapter 6.

- **Controls**: Any custom created controls land here. Typically, controls in here will be an inheritance of a Xamarin.Forms control so you can create a custom renderer for it.

- **Converters**: In this folder, I keep the value converters. More on this in Chapter 6.

- **DataTemplateSelectors**: This is where classes reside that act as `DataTemplate` selectors. You will see what this in more detail in Chapter 6.

- **Helpers**: Just like Santa, every good project needs some helpers. This is where they live. Not all classes in here will be handled in great detail. The `Settings` class is explained in Chapter 8.

- **Interfaces**: This folder contains all kinds of interface definitions. Mainly for use with the `DependencyService`, like you saw in Chapter 3.

- **Models**: Any models—classes that represent data—that you want to use in your app will be in here.

- **PageModels**: In this folder, you can find all the PageModels. All classes in here should have a one-on-one mapping with a counterpart in the `Pages` folder. The concept of pages and PageModels will be explained in this chapter when I talk about the MVVM pattern.

- **Pages**: All the pages of your application will be in this folder. This will be explained shortly. The pages are all the screens of your app.

- **Properties**: This is actually not a custom folder, but is added by Visual Studio. This contains files that specify the metadata—or properties—of the project.

- **Services**: Classes that provide you with data or connect to the backend I like to call *services* and they are placed in this folder. Communication with the backend is handled in Chapter 7.

- **Views**: To keep the pages clear and create reusable elements, you can create views. Basically, these contain a piece of XAML that can be placed in another page or view. More on this in Chapter 6.

Then, in the platform-specific project, these folders are included:

- **Extensions**: Not really a Xamarin.Forms concept, but in this folder, I keep my extension method classes.

- **Renderers**: Whenever custom renderers are needed, I put them in this folder. More on custom renderers in Chapter 4.

- **Resources**: For iOS and Android, this is where the resources are kept. Mostly these will contain the images that are used in your application. I describe this more extensively in Chapter 6.

- **Services**: Maybe this name isn't that great because of the Services folder in the shared project. The services folder on the platform project contains implementations of the interfaces for the DependencyService. In the past, I have also used the name *PlatformSpecifics*.

These names and this structure is how I like to set up the project, but in no way is the only way. You are free to choose other names or set it up completely differently.

Since namespaces are tied to folders in Visual Studio, it means that whenever you place something in one of these folders, they most likely have another namespace as well. To reference an element that's declared in another namespace in XAML, you need to declare the namespace in the root of your XAML file. For instance, if you want to use a control called `MyControl` in the `MyApp.Controls` namespace, you should add this attribute to the page you want to use it in: `<ContentPage xmlns:controls="clr-namespace:MyApp.Controls;assembly=MyApp.Core"><!--Your layout here --></ContentPage>`.

As you can see, we declare a new XML namespace (*xmlns*). The name can be anything; in this example, it's *controls*. Then as a value, you point to the namespace and optionally the assembly to find it in. This is optional, because when it lives in the same assembly, you can omit this. Otherwise, state the name of the DLL without the extension here. You can now use the control—or whatever it is you are trying to use from another namespace—like this: `<controls:MyControl PropertyName="PropertyValue" />`.

There is in fact another application that is needed for the complete "been pwned" app landscape. To be able to send push notifications, you need some server-side code. At the time of writing, this is not part of the new version yet. Also, this falls out of scope for this book and won't be handled explicitly.

Another thing you might want to do at some point is create a solution for each app platform. This solution includes the PCL project and just one app platform, like iOS. Of course, when there are more libraries that you require, you will need to add all of them into the solution as well.

When you are setting up a continuous integration pipeline, separate solutions are recommended. While you can set it up properly in one solution by setting up the configuration profiles the right way, it saves a lot of hassle to create one solution per app platform.

Using the MVVM Pattern

As I mentioned earlier, Xamarin.Forms is perfectly suited for implementing the MVVM pattern. If you are not familiar with it, read on.

What Is the MVVM Pattern?

MVVM stands for Model-View-ViewModel The pattern is derived from the Model-View-Controller (MVC) pattern. ASP.NET MVC is built entirely around this concept.

The MVVM pattern is an architectural pattern that enables you to separate business logic from UI code. While decoupling in code is always a good idea, using this pattern also allows you to easily swap views—even at runtime—and makes (unit) testing your code a lot easier.

As you may have surmised from the name, the pattern consists of three ingredients: Models, Views, and ViewModels. The ViewModel acts as an intermediary between the Model and the View. Figure 5-3 shows a schematic representation.

Figure 5-3. *A schematic overview of the MVVM pattern*

The ViewModel is responsible for converting values in a way that the View can present them to the user and is used to trigger business logic. To help you update the UI from the ViewModel, there is the concept of data binding, which I explain in a minute, and you will see more extensively later on.

To match mobile naming conventions better, I tend to use the terms *Page* and *PageModel*. Depending on who you are asking, they will use one of both variations. Just remember that wherever it reads Page or PageModel, you can replace it with View and ViewModel.

Using MVVM With Xamarin.Forms

Xamarin.Forms has a lot of ingredients that use MVVM right out of the box. This section highlights a couple of these right now. I will discuss them in-depth when we implement them into the application. For now, here are the main ingredients and how they are used:

- **View or Page**: This is the UI as seen by the user. Changes to the UI will be done through *data binding*, which is explained shortly. The page should not have any logic in itself, and if it does, the logic should only be used on UI elements, not to manipulate data or trigger business logic.

- **ViewModel or PageModel**: This acts as a proxy between calls to your business logic. You can trigger code by the use of *commands* from your page. The PageModel will contain a fair amount of properties that are necessary for data-binding the page.

- **Commands**: To avoid using the old-school events to trigger logic from the UI, commands were invented. Commands can be used as a property in your PageModel, and thus they can be used with data binding. This way you do not need any tight coupling between the UI and code that you might want to execute.

- • **Data binding**: This is used to decouple the UI from
  the rest of the code. The page has a property called
  DataContext, which takes in any object that will act
  as its PageModel. Then from that PageModel, any
  property can be used in a data binding on the UI. This
  is the way to show data and update the UI from code,
  without having to reference actual UI controls.

As an example, assume that you have a page called MyMvvmPage, which
contains the XAML from Listing 5-1.

Listing 5-1. The XAML Code for our MVVM Data Binding Example

```
<?xml version="1.0" encoding="utf-8"?>
<ContentPage xmlns="http://xamarin.com/schemas/2014/forms"
xmlns:x="http://schemas.microsoft.com/winfx/2009/xaml"
x:Class="Sample.MyMvvmPage">
    <Label Text="{Binding LabelText}" VerticalOptions="Center"
    HorizontalOptions="Center" />
</ContentPage>
```

Notice that the Text property of the Label does not contain a regular
value. Instead, the value is a data binding. To indicate a binding, it has to
be surrounded by curly braces and include Binding. The value after the
word Binding is the property in the PageModel that you want to use as the
value of this property—in this case, it's LabelText. You could also write it
like this:

```
{Binding Path=LabelText}
```

In a simple binding scenario, you can omit the Path= part. There are
several other options to be used in the data binding syntax, as you will see
later on.

Now look at the accompanying model called MyMvvmPageModel, shown
in Listing 5-2.

Listing 5-2. The PageModel for the MVVM Data Binding Example

```
public class MyMvvmPageModel
{
        public string LabelText { get; set; } = "Hello from the
        PageModel!";
}
```

This is a very simple model; real-life models will usually be a lot more complex. In the code for the MyMvvmPageModel, you will see the LabelText property, which was mentioned in the page. The value of this property is the value of the Label's Text property. Note that this *has* to be a property! It will not work with fields.

Now you just need one line of code to tie these two together. In the code-behind of the MyMvvmPage, we add the code of Listing 5-3 to the constructor.

Listing 5-3. Setting the BindingContext Property to Complete the Data Binding

```
public MyMvvmPage()
{
        InitializeComponent();

        var pageModel = new MyMvvmPageModel();

        BindingContext = pageModel;
}
```

What you see happening here is that I instantiate a new MyMvvmPageModel and set that as the value of the MyMvvmPage's BindingContext property. Whenever the BindingContext is set, all the data bindings are evaluated and each binding in the page is replaced with the actual value at that time.

Notice how the values are evaluated only at that time. It will not be a very uncommon situation that you want to update the values and let the user interface reflect these changes in values. To do this, you need to implement the INotifyPropertyChanged interface. By implementing this interface, you introduce some infrastructure to notify the UI that a change has been made to a value. The control(s) bound to the property for which this signal is raised will then be updated accordingly. Listing 5-4 shows the updated PageModel code with the implementation of the INotifyPropertyChanged interface.

Listing 5-4. Implementing the INotifyPropertyChanged Interface to Update Data Binding Values

```
public class MyMvvmPageModel : INotifyPropertyChanged
{
        private string _labelText = "Hello from the
        PageModel!";
        public string LabelText
        {
                get
                {
                        return _labelText;
                }

                set
                {
                        _labelText = value;
                        PropertyChanged?.Invoke(this, new
                        PropertyChangedEventArgs(nameof
                        (LabelText)));
                }
        }
```

```
    public event PropertyChangedEventHandler
    PropertyChanged;
}
```

Notice how a new event was introduced: PropertyChanged. When the UI detects that the INotifyPropertyChanged interface is implemented, it will automatically hook into this event. Then whenever a property is updated, you need to call this event to let the subscribers know that the value of this property has changed. You see this happening in the set handler of the LabelText property.

The last thing I want to cover is the use of commands. Using commands is very similar to what we did above, because it is handled just the same.

In Listing 5-5, I added a Button in the MyMvvmPage.

Listing 5-5. Button Added to the MyMvvmPage

```xml
<?xml version="1.0" encoding="utf-8"?>
<ContentPage xmlns="http://xamarin.com/schemas/2014/forms"
        xmlns:x="http://schemas.microsoft.com/winfx/2009/xaml"
        xmlns:local="clr-namespace:DncMvvm" x:Class="Sample.
        MyMvvmPage">

    <StackLayout VerticalOptions="Center" Horizontal
    Options="Center">
            <Label Text="{Binding LabelText}" />
            <Button Text="Knock, knock..."
            Command="{Binding KnockCommand}" />
    </StackLayout>
</ContentPage>
```

You can see how the Button has a Command property. This property can be used to bind to a type—also called a Command—which can execute code. Listing 5-6 shows how the PageModel is updated accordingly.

Listing 5-6. Implementing the Command

```
public class MyMvvmPageModel : INotifyPropertyChanged
{
        private string _labelText = "Hello from the
        PageModel!";
        public string LabelText
        {
                get
                {
                        return _labelText;
                }

                set
                {
                        _labelText = value;
                        PropertyChanged?.Invoke(this, new
                        PropertyChangedEventArgs(nameof
                        (LabelText)));
                }
        }

        public Command KnockCommand { get; }

        public MyMvvmPageModel()
        {
                KnockCommand = new Command(() =>
                {
                        LabelText = "Who's there?";
                });
        }

        public event PropertyChangedEventHandler Property
        Changed;
}
```

The PageModel includes a new property called KnockCommand. This command is wired up in the PageModel constructor. The parameter of the Command takes a method of lambda expression with code that has to be executed whenever the Command is called upon. In this case, the text of the LabelText property will be changed and, because the INotifyPropertyChanged interface is implemented, the value will be updated in the UI.

Tip   When you start working with Xamarin.Forms more intensively, you could encounter a control that does not support commands. There are solutions available to turn an event into a command, because you want to avoid events at any cost when using MVVM. Read more on how to do this in this blog post by Xamarin: https://blog.xamarin.com/turn-events-into-commands-with-behaviors/.

Commands have an additional functionality you should know about. They also have a CanExecute property. As a second parameter when instantiating the command, you can add an expression that determines whether a command can be executed at some point in time. For example, when a signup form is being evaluated server-side, you set some boolean that indicates that a loading operation is in progress. By setting that boolean, the command will set the CanExecute to false. If the control implemented it right, the control will look and be disabled at that time. In practice, I find myself not using it all too much, but I thought it would be useful for you to know about.

While data binding is handled more extensively later in this book when we start building the screens, you can also read more on the Xamarin documentation pages: https://developer.xamarin.com/guides/xamarin-forms/xaml/xaml-basics/data_binding_basics/.

Using a MVVM Framework

To separate the UI and your logic, you also do not want to reference another page when navigating. Implementing MVVM the right way also means that you want to implement `PageModel` to `PageModel` navigation. This means that when you need to navigate to another screen, you would rather want to tell your application to which `PageModel` it should navigate and not the page it should navigate to. If we were to navigate to a page, we would still have a reference to pages and implementing a new view would mean that we have to change code.

This is just one of the features that is not included by default in Xamarin.Forms. So, the preparations are there but some gaps are still there. I don't think this is due to Xamarin not wanting to implement these features, but more due to the fact that every developer wants to do things like navigation their own way.

That is why there are a lot of different MVVM frameworks out there. These frameworks provide you with just that little bit extra that you need to implement clean MVVM. Among these frameworks are MvvmCross, which dates back from before Xamarin and only supports Xamarin. Forms recently at the time of writing. Prism, MvvmLight, and Caliburn. Micro were all developed long before Xamarin. Another great one worth mentioning is from my friend Adam Pedley, called Exrin. There are a lot of others out there, again because developers like to do things their own way.

I like to use FreshMvvm. This framework is developed by Michael Ridland and is designed specifically with Xamarin.Forms in mind. The main differentiator between all these frameworks is whether the framework is designed for Xamarin.Forms or merely adapted to work with Forms?

Because Xamarin.Forms already has a lot on-board in regards to using the MVVM pattern, I tend to like frameworks that are designed specifically for Xamarin.Forms. They just complement the missing pieces.

For the "been pwned" app, I choose FreshMvvm. Here's a quick overview of the features as listed on the project page, which can be found at `https://github.com/rid00z/FreshMvvm`. The main features in the app are the following:

- `PageModel` to `PageModel` navigation

- Automatic wiring of `BindingContext`

- Automatic wiring of `Page` events (e.g., appearing)

- Basic methods (with values) on `PageModel` (`init`, `reverseinit`)

- Built-in IOC container

- `PageModel` Constructor Injection

- Basic methods available in `Model`, like `Alert`

- Built-in Navigation types for `SimpleNavigation`, `Tabbed`, and `MasterDetail`

I don't cover all of them in detail here, as you will see how it works in the next chapter. The one thing that I do want to point out here is that FreshMvvm uses convention over configuration. This means that you do not need any code to map the pages to the PageModels. As long as you keep the naming consistent, FreshMvvm will automatically understand which page belongs to which `PageModel`. This is the same convention I have been using throughout this chapter: the page will be named as `IdentifierPage`, where `identifier` has to be a self-describing name for the page. The `PageModel` should then be named `IdentifierPageModel`, where `identifier` is the same as the one used for the page.

FreshMvvm also includes an IOC container, which stands for Inversion of Control. This is another pattern that can be used to decouple your code. Basically, it means that you define an interface for classes that other classes have a dependency on. We have seen this kind of behavior in the

DependencyService. By wrapping the dependency classes in interfaces, you can register any implementation of that interface if you might need different behavior.

Then, you *inject* that interface through the constructor of the dependent class. That way, the dependent class does not have to have a hard reference to the class that implements the logic you need. By solving it with the IOC pattern (also known as Dependency Injection—DI), you can easily swap out one implementation with the other, without having to touch any other code. A quick example of how this works is shown in Listing 5-7.

Listing 5-7. Quick Example of IOC at Work in FreshMvvm

```
// Register an interface with its implementing class
FreshIOC.Container.Register<IDatabaseService,
DatabaseService>();

// Resolve the implementation manually...
FreshIOC.Container.Resolve<IDatabaseService>();

// ... Or use PageModel construction injection
public class SamplePageModel
{
        private IDatabaseService _databaseService;

        public SamplePageModel (IDatabaseService
        databaseService)
        {
                _databaseService = databaseService;
        }
}
```

Using a MVVM framework is not necessary, but it can make your life a whole lot easier.

Summary

Using MVVM with Xamarin.Forms is the most obvious choice. Especially when it's combined with a complementary MVVM framework, apps can be built lightning fast.

For the "been pwned" app, I will make no exception and take advantage of MVVM. I like to use the FreshMvvm framework in almost all of my projects because it has a straightforward API and is very lightweight—it just adds some missing parts.

With this chapter I hope you have a better understanding of how the app will be built and how MVVM works. In addition, it also explained how IOC works, what other MVVM frameworks are out there, and how to start a blank Xamarin.Forms application from Visual Studio.

In the next chapter, you start building the screens. It will guide you through building most of the application screens and, while doing so, it will go deeper into the concepts you learned about in this chapter.

CHAPTER 6

Building Screens

This chapter goes in-depth into the key aspects of the "been pwned" app. By looking at the screens and how they are built, you will see how Xamarin. Forms features and concepts are implemented.

Because describing every line of every page in detail might be a bit much, I selected the ones that have the most interesting elements. The remainder of the pages have variations of those same elements.

The Main Entry Point

To start the app, we have the `App.xaml` and `App.xaml.cs` files. The latter is actually most important. In fact, the `App.xaml` page can be removed altogether. Although this is not an actual screen by itself, this is a very important class. It consists of a XAML page and a code-behind file. Let's start with the XAML part. Listing 6-1 shows an abbreviated version of the `App.xaml` file.

Listing 6-1. The App.xaml File for the Been Pwned App

```xml
<?xml version="1.0" encoding="utf-8"?>
<Application xmlns="http://xamarin.com/schemas/2014/forms"
    xmlns:x="http://schemas.microsoft.com/winfx/2009/xaml"
    xmlns:local="clr-namespace:BeenPwned.App.Core.Controls;
    assembly=BeenPwned.App.Core"
```

```xml
    xmlns:converters="clr-namespace:BeenPwned.App.Core.
    Converters;assembly=BeenPwned.App.Core"
    x:Class="BeenPwned.App.BeenPwnedApp">
        <Application.Resources>
            <ResourceDictionary>
            <converters:BreachToImageUrlConverter x:Key="Breach
            ToImageUrlConverter" />

                <!-- Our custom colors -->
                <Color x:Key="MainTextColor">#444444</Color>
                <Color x:Key="SecondaryTextColor">#666666
                </Color>
                <Color x:Key="PageBackgroundColor">#FFFFFF
                </Color>

                <!-- Styles for common elements -->
            <Style TargetType="Label">
                <Setter Property="FontFamily">
                    <Setter.Value>
                      <OnPlatform x:TypeArguments="x:String">
                        <On Platform="iOS" Value="Ubuntu-
                        Regular" />
                      </OnPlatform>
                    </Setter.Value>
                </Setter>
                <Setter Property="FontSize" Value="14" />
                <Setter Property="TextColor"
                Value="{StaticResource MainTextColor}" />
            </Style>
          </ResourceDictionary>
          </Application.Resources>
</Application>
```

As you can see, this is not an actual screen, but it acts more like a general file for gathering styling entries. This is also apparent by the root node for this XAML file. It does not mention a page of any kind; instead it is denoted as an `Application`.

Styling

One thing I did not mention yet is that Xamarin.Forms also has support for styling. At this level, you can define resources in a `ResourceDictionary`. This can be multiple things, such as a converter being declared. The `BreachToImageUrlConverter` is a value converter.

Then you can see a couple of colors being defined. By defining them like this, you don't have to go through the entire app when you want to change the base color. When you now need to change a color, you change it in the `App.xaml` file and it will automatically change at all the places where you referenced it. You can use the color at any property of a control that takes a color like this: `<ContentPage BackgroundColor="{Static Resource PageBackgroundColor}" />`.

In the last part of the file is a `Style` entry. This enables you to define a whole style for controls. You can define them either *implicitly* or *explicitly*. If you look at the style defined in Listing 6-1, you will see that a `Label` control is being styled. With each `Setter`, one property of the `Label` is being set to a certain value. In this style, the font, font size, and text color are all set.

Because the style does not have an `x:Key` property—similar to the converter which does have one—this is an *implicit* style. This means that this style will be applied to all the `Label` controls in the app. If you gave the style a key, for instance `LabelStyle`, then you would have to apply it to the `Label` controls manually, like this: `<Label Style="{StaticResource LabelStyle}" />`. This is called an *explicit* style, because you have to apply it explicitly.

Cascading Resource Dictionaries

When you define resources in the `ResourceDictionary` at the application-level, you have access to them on all pages. Although this might come in handy for resources that you use on multiple pages, that might not always be what you want. You can also define your resources on other levels, like on your page or even in your custom control. Note that the level you define the resources on limits the scope. If you put it on the control level, the resources are only available for that control and its children, for example.

You can cascade them by defining a resource at one level and another resource at another level. If you choose to use the same key for a resource, the one at the lowest level will override the one above. You can also merge dictionaries. That way ,you can structure the different styling elements apart for a better overview. At the time of this writing, only one dictionary merge was allowed. However, a pull request was added to the Xamarin. Forms repository, which adds multiple merged dictionaries. Hopefully this will be part of Xamarin.Forms by the time this book is published.

Platform-Specific XAML or Code

The last thing to note in the XAML is the `OnPlatform` tag. While Xamarin. Forms intends to be a unified way of constructing your user interface, each platform still has its own behavior. A nice example of this is the status bar for iOS and Android. The status bar is at the top of the screen and indicates your battery level, etc. On iOS, the status bar is part of the screen and you can put your controls and whatnot behind it if you want. Android, on the other hand, starts drawing at the bottom of the status bar. So, in your UI, you might want to have a difference of padding. If you don't, iOS will draw behind the status bar and Android will look fine, but if you specify a padding, iOS will look fine, but Android will show a gap between the status bar and your content.

To overcome this, Xamarin has introduced the OnPlatform tag. With this tag, you can use different values for each platform. In Listing 6-1, it's used to set a custom font for iOS, but it does not specify a value for another platform explicitly. If that is the case, the default value is used on that platform. Another example is shown in Listing 6-2. It shows the XAML needed to solve the status bar problem I described earlier.

Listing 6-2. Adding Separate Padding Values for iOS and Android

```
<ContentPage xmlns="http://xamarin.com/schemas/2014/forms"
             xmlns:x="http://schemas.microsoft.com/winfx/
             2009/xaml"
             x:Class="Sample.PaddingOnPlatform">
  <ContentPage.Padding>
    <OnPlatform x:TypeArguments="Thickness">
      <On Platform ="iOS" Value="0,20,0,0" />
      <On Platform="Android" Value="0,0,0,0" />
    </OnPlatform>
  </ContentPage.Padding>
  ...
</ContentPage>
```

Note that we did not have to specify a value for Android here, but for clarity, I did add it to this example. You can use this method for all properties on all XAML tags.

You can do this from code as well. This functionality is not to be confused with the DependencyService you saw in Chapter 3. The DependencyService is used to access platform-specific code, and with this method we can execute different code depending on the platform. You won't be able to access platform-specifics from there since you are still in the shared code.

Listing 6-3 shows you how you can detect the current platform.

Listing 6-3. Detecting the Platform Running in Code

```
switch(Device.RuntimePlatform)
{
    case Device.iOS:
        MainPage.BackgroundColor = Color.Black;
        break;
    case Device.Android:
        MainPage.BackgroundColor = Color.Red;
        break;
default:
        MainPage.BackgroundColor = Color.Transparent;
        break;
}
```

Now that we have handled everything there is to see in the App.xaml file, let's look at the code-behind in the App.xaml.cs file. The contents are shown in Listing 6-4.

Listing 6-4. Contents of the App.xaml.cs File

```
[assembly: XamlCompilation(XamlCompilationOptions.Compile)]
namespace BeenPwned.App
{
    public partial class BeenPwnedApp : Application
    {
        public static BeenPwnedApp Instance;

        public BeenPwnedApp()
        {
            InitializeComponent();

            BlobCache.ApplicationName = "BeenPwned";
```

```
    Instance = this;

    if (!Settings.Current.SkippedTutorial)
    {
        var page = FreshPageModelResolver.ResolvePage
        Model<TutorialPageModel>();

        MainPage = new FreshNavigationContainer(page)
        {
            BarTextColor = Color.White,
            BarBackgroundColor = Color.FromHex
            ("#3a9ac4"),
        };
    }
    else
    {
        SwitchToMainPage();
    }
}

public void SwitchToMainPage()
{
    var tabbed = new FreshTabbedNavigationContainer();

    tabbed.AddTab<MainPageModel>("Been pwned?",
    "icon-pwned.png");
    tabbed.AddTab<BreachesPageModel>("Breaches",
    "icon-breaches.png");
    tabbed.AddTab<PasswordPageModel>("Passwords",
    "icon-password.png");

    MainPage = tabbed;
}
```

```
    protected override void OnStart()
    {
        // Handle when your app starts
    }

    protected override void OnSleep()
    {
        // Handle when your app sleeps
    }

    protected override void OnResume()
    {
        // Handle when your app resumes
    }
  }
}
```

There is a lot going on here; let's start with the top-level methods and drill down from there.

XAML Compilation

Actually, there is something interesting happening on the very first line; there is an attribute called XamlCompilation. Check out the [assembly: XamlCompilation(XamlCompilationOptions.Compile)] line. This enables the compilation of XAML pages. By default, XAML pages are interpreted at runtime. That means that whenever you made a typo or entered invalid XAML, you will only detect it when you run your application. With XAML compilation your pages will be parsed at compile-time and the compiler will let you know if there is any error. There are a couple of other advantages as well:

- The XAML will already be compiled, so the time to instantiate and load XAML elements is removed when XAML compilation is enabled.

- With XAML compilation enabled, the final assembly will have a smaller file size since the XAML files are no longer included.

- As mentioned, errors are detected at compile-time.

By adding the `assembly` prefix to the attribute, all the XAML that resides in that assembly is compiled. You can also choose to include only certain pages or elements by moving the attribute to that class and removing the `assembly` prefix. There is also a `XamlCompilationOptions.Skip` option. This can be used to skip compilation of a certain page or element. These options can be used together: you can enable XAML compilation of the whole assembly, but exclude certain pages with the skip option.

Application Lifecycle Methods

Now let's look at the methods that are shown in Listing 6-4, namely `OnStart`, `OnSleep`, and `OnResume`. These methods are wired to the events on each platform and are fired whenever the app is started, sent to the background, or brought back from the background. While these events are available on nearly every platform right now, they are implemented in different ways across the platforms. Xamarin.Forms unites these events for you. There is no method available for when the app is terminated, simply because there is no (reliable) signal from the different platforms for this. Normally, when the app is terminated it will come through the `OnSleep` method, but there are no guarantees. Also, this will not happen when the app crashes.

In the "been pwned" app, these methods have no implementation, simply because we didn't have any use for it.

Wrapping Up the App Class

The most logic in the entry point of this app happens in the constructor. There are two things that I will handle later on: the line where I set the name for the `BlobCache` and the line where I evaluate the `Settings` object. These are both a plugin that I use, which is described more extensively in Chapter 8.

What globally happens is that you determine which page to show. The current page of the app is determined by a property called `MainPage` in the App object. We implemented a kind of tutorial page where we show the user the features of our app, and then of course when the user has reviewed that, we show the actual app. These pages are shown in Figure 6-1.

 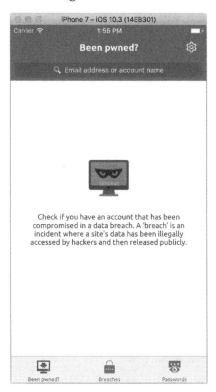

Figure 6-1. *On the left the tutorial page, on the right the actual main page of the app*

Most of the time you would just set the `MainPage` property once and navigate throughout the app from there. However, it is possible to replace the whole main page. For instance, like we did with the tutorial page here, or when the user is required to log in through a login page.

Furthermore, there are a couple of lines of code that have the word `Fresh` in them. These have to do with the usage of the FreshMvvm framework I told you about in Chapter 5. For instance, this line: `FreshPageModelResolver.ResolvePageModel<TutorialPageModel>();`. Because we do not want to reference actual pages, we will sometimes have to resolve the page that belongs to a certain `PageModel`. When you navigate normally, FreshMvvm will do this for you. But, when you need the page that belongs to a certain `PageModel`, you can resolve it at that time.

In the `SwitchToMainPage` method, you can see how we construct the app's main page and show it to the user by setting that value as the `MainPage` of our app. Just like Xamarin.Forms, FreshMvvm has some built-in layouts as well. This is required to enable the automatic wiring of the `BindingContext`. If you have to manually create a tabbed page and add each page to a tab, you also have to set the binding context for it. By using FreshMvvm's `FreshTabbedNavigationContainer`, you can add tabs as `PageModel`s and the page is located automatically. With the `AddTab` calls, you add each PageModel as a new tab and set a label and icon to show on platforms that support this.

While this tabbed page is the actual main screen for the app, we won't handle it individually since it is only a container for the other pages. We will now start looking at the rest of the pages in the app to see what concepts we can find there.

The Been Pwned? Page

The page in the first tab allows the user to search the records to see if their account was part of any hack. A hack will also be referred to as a *breach*. Another type of record that is also indexed by Troy Hunt on `haveibeenpwned.com` are *pastes*. It is very common among hackers to

dump the contents of a hack on sites like `pastebin.com`, which allow users
to upload text files anonymously. Because of that, these kinds of web sites
are used to publish breached accounts as well. These records can also be
searched through the HIBP APIs and are therefore included in our app as
well. This page, with search results, is shown in Figure 6-2.

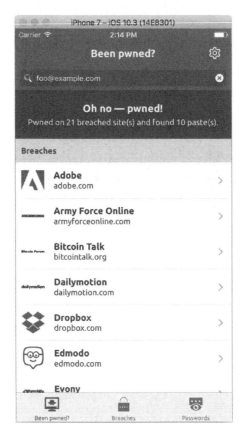

Figure 6-2. *The Been pwned? page of the application showing search
results*

Before you look at the code behind this, try to identify the different
elements. You can see a `SearchBar`, some block to indicate that this user
has been pwned, and a `ListView` to show the results.

Because the layout for this page is quite verbose, I have outlined the XAML definition of this page in a simpler form in Listing 6-5, just showing the top nodes. I will then walk you through the specifics of each element. This code, in full, can be viewed at `https://github.com/jfversluis/been-pwned/blob/master/src/BeenPwnedApp/Core/Pages/MainPage.xaml`.

Listing 6-5. Simplified Overview of the Been Pwned? Page in XAML

```
<ContentPage.Content>
    <Grid RowSpacing="0" ColumnSpacing="0">
        <Grid.RowDefinitions>
            <RowDefinition Height="40" />
            <RowDefinition Height="Auto" />
            <RowDefinition Height="*" />
        </Grid.RowDefinitions>

        <SearchBar Placeholder="Email address or account name" />

        <StackLayout IsVisible="{Binding HasSearched}"
        Padding="20" Grid.Row="1">
            <Label Text="Good news – no pwnage found!" />
            <Label Text="No breached accounts." />
        </StackLayout>

        <StackLayout IsVisible="{Binding HasItems}"
        Padding="20" Grid.Row="1">
            <Label Text="Oh no – pwned!" />
            <Label Text="{Binding BreachedDescription}" />
        </StackLayout>

        <StackLayout IsVisible="{Binding HasItems,
        Converter={StaticResource InverseBoolConverter}}" Grid.
        Row="2">
            <Image Source="icon-pwned-color.png" />
```

```
            <Label Text="Check if you have an account,,," />
        </StackLayout>

        <ListView Grid.Row="2" x:Name="BreachesList"
        ItemsSource="{Binding BreachesAndPastes}">
            <ListView.Behaviors>
                <behaviors:ListViewSelectedItemBehavior
                Command="{Binding OpenBreachCommand}" />
            </ListView.Behaviors>
             <ListView.GroupHeaderTemplate>
                <DataTemplate>
                    <ViewCell Height="40">

                        ...

                    </ViewCell>
                </DataTemplate>
            </ListView.GroupHeaderTemplate>
        </ListView>

        <views:LoadingView IsVisible="{Binding IsLoading}"/>
        <views:ErrorView  IsVisible="{Binding IsError}"/>
    </Grid>
</ContentPage.Content>
```

As you can see, the elements identified earlier are all there. There is however one that isn't—the top navigation bar.

NavigationPage

The bar with the Been Pwned? title in Figure 6-2 has the cog icon in it. This bar appears because the pages are wrapped in a NavigationPage. When pages are used together with a NavigationPage, a bar will appear at the top and will hold the Back button if needed. It can also hold toolbar icons. Because we used the FreshTabbedNavigationContainer, which comes with FreshMvvm, all child pages of the tabbed page are automatically wrapped in a NavigationPage. When you navigate to another page, for example by clicking one of the options in the ListView, a back button appears in that bar. This back button is automatically handled by the operating system on the phone. The navigation bar also allows you to use toolbar icons, like the one shown in Figure 6-2 with the cogwheel icon.

To declare an icon, use the ToolbarItems collection on a page. Listing 6-6 shows you a simple page that uses a toolbar icon.

Listing 6-6. Simple Use of the ToolbarItems Collection

```xml
<?xml version="1.0" encoding="UTF-8"?>
<ContentPage xmlns="http://xamarin.com/schemas/2014/forms"
xmlns:x="http://schemas.microsoft.com/winfx/2009/xaml"
x:Class="BeenPwned.App.Core.Pages.BasePage">
    <ContentPage.ToolbarItems>
        <ToolbarItem Icon="icon-settings.png" Text="Settings"
        Command="{Binding OpenSettingsCommand}" />
    </ContentPage.ToolbarItems>
</ContentPage>
```

Listing 6-6 is the code that is used to create the cogwheel icon in Figure 6-2. But imagine that this was a standalone page. Normally, you would wrap this page in a NavigationPage, using MainPage = new NavigationPage(new BasePage());. You can now navigate like you would normally and the OS will handle the stack for you.

Adding resources like the icon and other app metadata is explained at the end of this chapter.

Grid

Let's go back to the actual page in Listing 6-5. At the top level, a grid is defined. We use this grid to divide the screen into three rows—one has a height of 40, one has a height of auto, and the last row is *. In Figure 6-3, you can see the grid over the actual layout.

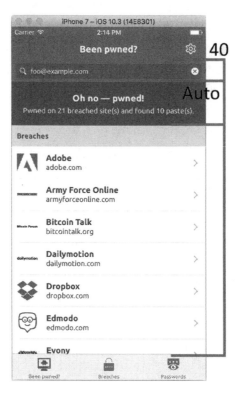

Figure 6-3. *Grid layout shown on the actual screen*

The same way we divided the screen into different rows, you could do that for columns, or use both. The numeric value for a height (or width, when using columns) is pretty self-explanatory, but the values auto and * need some more explaining. Here's how those values are set:

- **Auto**: Lets the children decide what the width or height is.

- **Proportional (*)**: You set the size as a proportion of the remaining space. When you use just *, this column or row will take up all the remaining space. You could also add a number in front of the asterisk to make it proportional, for example: 2*.

- **Absolute**: When you enter a numeric value, it's use used as an absolute value in pixels.

If you translate this back to the screen in Figure 6-3, you can see that the SeachBar has a fixed height of 40, the red Pwned Results Box has a height that is determined by its children, and the ListView will take up the rest of the remaining space.

The elements that can be used inside a row or column of a grid is basically any visual element, including other layout elements. To place an element inside a certain column or row—or both, if you combine them—set the Grid.Row or Grid.Column property similar to this: <Label Text="I'm in the second row and the third column" Grid.Row="1" Grid.Column="2" />.

As you can see, the row and column index start at 0. If you do not explicitly set the row or column, a default value of 0 will be used.

Finally, if we look back at the definition of the grid, you see two more properties: RowSpacing and ColumnSpacing. With these properties, you can specify how much space there should be between the columns or rows.

SearchBar

Next, we look at the SearchBar. The full code is shown in Listing 6-7.

Listing 6-7. The Full Code of the SearchBar

```
<SearchBar BackgroundColor="{StaticResource
NavigationBackgroundColor}" CancelButtonColor="White" Grid.
Row="0" TextColor="White" PlaceholderColor="White"
Placeholder="Email address or account name" FontSize="13"
Text="{Binding Filter}" SearchCommand="{Binding
CheckPwnedCommand}" HeightRequest="40" />
```

With the SearchBar element, you will be provided with an input field focused on searching. Typically, it is attached to the navigation bar, but doesn't have to be. It implements some functionality to clear the text and show a Cancel button when the user has performed a search action.

In the implementation in the "been pwned" app, you see a couple of concepts you learned before. The BackgroundColor is set through a value in the application's ResourceDictionary; the SearchBar sits in the first row of the grid; then there are couple of data bindings in the Text and SearchCommand properties. Let's go through a couple of interesting things about the SearchBar. The most notable thing is probably that a search is only triggered when the user presses the search button on their keyboard. When they do, the command that is bound to the SearchCommand property is invoked.

The Command in this case executes the search and fills the ListView with the results. Depending on these results—or better yet, if there are any results, some booleans are flipped to show the right views. More on this a little later.

StackLayout

Then there are a couple of StackLayouts on the page. Since they are pretty similar, I show only the most advanced one. The full code is shown in Listing 6-8.

Listing 6-8. The Full Code of the StackLayout on the MainPage

```
<StackLayout IsVisible="{Binding HasItems,
Converter={StaticResource InverseBoolConverter}}" Grid.
Row="2" Padding="20,0,20,0" VerticalOptions="Center"
Margin="0,-40,0,0">
```

```
<Image Source="icon-pwned-color.png" HorizontalOptions=
"Center" Margin="0,0,0,10" />
<Label Margin="0,0,0,30" HorizontalTextAlignment=
"Center" Text="Check if you have an account that has been
compromised in a data breach. A 'breach' is an incident
where a site's data has been illegally accessed by hackers
and then released publicly." />
</StackLayout>
```

Most of the code shown here you've already seen. It is a StackLayout, so you know that each child you put in there will simply be stacked on the rest. Together with the VerticalOptions and HorizontalOptions properties, the content is centered in the screen.

The most interesting thing here is in the IsVisible property of the StackLayout. You see a regular binding, but it also has a converter. This is where the IValueConverter comes in.

The concept of value converters is pretty straightforward. You create a class that implements the IValueConverter, which makes you implement the Convert and ConvertBack methods. With these methods, you can take any kind of object and write your own logic to transform it into any other object. How this exactly works we will see in a moment. Also, this concept isn't specific to Xamarin; you will also find it in other applications that can leverage the MVVM pattern.

In this case, however, it's not used to transform the data bound value to another type, but it is used to invert it. The value of the HasItems property in the PageModel is inverted. This is done so this particular StackLayout is not shown whenever there are search results.

Listing 6-9 shows the implementation of the InverseBoolConverter.

Listing 6-9. Implementation of the InverseBoolConverter

```
public class InverseBoolConverter : IValueConverter
{
    public object Convert(object value, Type targetType, object
    parameter, System.Globalization.CultureInfo culture)
    {
        return !(bool)value;
    }
    public object ConvertBack(object value, Type targetType,
    object parameter, System.Globalization.CultureInfo culture)
    {
        return !(bool)value;
    }
}
```

We could also have chosen to create an additional property in the PageModel with the inverse value, but this seems a bit more elegant.

The more common scenario here is to transfer one type to another. Somewhere else in the "been pwned" app, we check if the added date of the breach is today and if it is, we show that the breach is new. You can see the implementation at https://github.com/jfversluis/been-pwned/blob/master/src/BeenPwnedApp/Core/Converters/DateToVisibleConverter.cs. An implementation like this would be more common.

But this doesn't matter for the concept of the IValueConverter. Let's go back to the two methods that need to be implemented for this interface. As you could've guessed, this is for the conversion back and forth. It isn't uncommon that the ConvertBack is not implemented. For instance, the example in Listing 6-9 implements the ConvertBack, but it will never be called upon. We might just as well have throw new NotImplementedException(); in there.

The thing you need to know about value converters is that you have to pay attention to casting your values right. You get a general object in and have to return a general object as well, so make sure these are the expected types from and to your page's binding.

Lastly, make sure that you declare the converter in your ResourceDictionary with a key at some level so you can reference to it from the binding.

That is basically everything you need to know about value converters. For a more standalone example, look at my blog post at https://1.verslu.is/2sBS4wb.

ListView

To view the search results, there is a ListView control in place. The full code for the ListView is shown in Listing 6-10.

Listing 6-10. The Full Code for the ListView

```
<ListView IsVisible="{Binding HasItems}" Grid.Row="2"
x:Name="BreachesList" ItemsSource="{Binding
BreachesAndPastes}" HasUnevenRows="true"
IsGroupingEnabled="true" GroupDisplayBinding="{Binding Name}"
ItemTemplate="{StaticResource breachOrPasteTemplateSelector}"
SeparatorColor="{StaticResource ListSeparatorColor}" >
    <ListView.Behaviors>
        <behaviors:ListViewSelectedItemBehavior
        Command="{Binding OpenBreachCommand}" />
    </ListView.Behaviors>
    <ListView.GroupHeaderTemplate>
      <DataTemplate>
          <ViewCell Height="40">
```

```
        <ContentView VerticalOptions="FillAndExpand"
        BackgroundColor="{StaticResource Section
        GroupBackgroundColor}">
            <Label Style="{StaticResource BoldLabel}"
            Margin="10,0,0,0" Text="{Binding Name}"
            TextColor="{StaticResource
            SectionGroupTextColor}" VerticalTextAlignment
            ="Center"/>
        </ContentView>
      </ViewCell>
    </DataTemplate>
  </ListView.GroupHeaderTemplate>
</ListView>
```

There is a lot going on in this piece of code. I skip over the bindings and obvious stuff that you know by now. There are a couple of interesting properties to mention here. The most important one is the ItemsSource. This is where the list gets its items. It can be any type of collection, but you probably want to use the ObservableCollection if you want to update the items in the list. With the ObservableCollection, you can add and remove items from the list, and those actions will be reflected in the ListView automatically. The important point to remember here is that you do not create a new instance of the ObservableCollection; instead you empty it or add/remove items.

With the HasUnevenRows property, you specify that the rows in the ListView are not necessarily the same height. When the HasUnevenRows property is set to true, the height of each row will automatically be calculated.

Furthermore, this particular list has grouping enabled. This can be done by setting IsGroupingEnabled to true. This will add a header row for each group. For this, you need to specify what value is to be used as the group title by setting the GroupDisplayBinding. To make this behavior

possible, you need to use a special kind of collection as your ItemsSource.
The source does not just need to be a list of items that you want to show,
but you need add an extra dimension to your collection. You can do this
by extending a collection and adding your own properties to support this.
Another option is to use the Grouping type in the mvvm-helpers plugin by
James Montemagno. I explain more about this in Chapter 8.

DataTemplates and DataTemplateSelector

To format the items being shown in the list, you can use a DataTemplate.
In a simpler scenario, you could specify the template that is to be used for
each item in the list, like ListView.GroupHeaderTemplate is defined now.
With GroupHeaderTemplate and ItemTemplate, you basically design a
layout that will be used for the group headers and for each separate item in
the list, respectively. Note that the scope of the data binding shifts here.

Within a template, the scope will be the item that is bound to that
particular cell. In the code in Listing 6-10, you see that the ItemTemplate is
set to a resource that has the key breachOrPasteTemplateSelector. As you
can deduce from the name, this is a DataTemplateSelector. This enables
you to implement logic to determine what template to use in for a given
cell in the ListView. The way to do this is to declare one or more templates
in your resources, along with a template selector. In Listing 6-11, you can
see the resources as they are defined in the MainPage.xaml.

Listing 6-11. Resources in the MainPage.xaml File

```
<ContentPage.Resources>
    <ResourceDictionary>
        <DataTemplate x:Key="breachCellTemplate">
            <local:AccessoryViewCell Accessory="disclosure">
                <Grid HeightRequest="60">
                    <Grid.ColumnDefinitions>
                        <ColumnDefinition Width="60" />
```

```
                    <ColumnDefinition Width="*" />
                    <ColumnDefinition Width="Auto" />
                </Grid.ColumnDefinitions>
                <ContentView Grid.Column="0">
                    <ffimageloadingsvg:SvgC
                    achedImage Margin="10"
                    HeightRequest="40" WidthRequest="80"
                    DownsampleToViewSize="true"
                    Source="{Binding .,
                    Converter={StaticResource
                    BreachToImageUrlConverter}}">
                        <ffimageloadingsvg:SvgCachedImage.
                        Transformations>
                            <transformations:Sele
                            ctiveTintTransformati
                            on HexColor="#ff000000"
                            EnableSolidColor="true" />
                        </ffimageloadingsvg:SvgCachedImage.
                        Transformations>
                    </ffimageloadingsvg:SvgCachedImage>
                </ContentView>
                <StackLayout VerticalOptions="Center"
                Grid.Column="1">
                    <Label Margin="0,5,0,0" FontSize="16"
                    Style="{StaticResource BoldLabel}"
                    Text="{Binding Title}" />
                    <Label Margin="0,-5,0,5" Text="{Binding
                    Domain}" />
                </StackLayout>
            </Grid>
        </local:AccessoryViewCell>
```

```
        </DataTemplate>
        <DataTemplate x:Key="pasteCellTemplate">
            <local:AccessoryViewCell Accessory="disclosure">
                <Grid HeightRequest="60">
                    <Grid.ColumnDefinitions>
                        <ColumnDefinition Width="*" />
                        <ColumnDefinition Width="Auto" />
                    </Grid.ColumnDefinitions>
                    <StackLayout VerticalOptions="Center" Grid.
                    Column="0">
                        <Label Margin="20,5,0,0" FontSize="16"
                        Style="{StaticResource BoldLabel}"
                        Text="{Binding Source}" />
                        <Label Margin="20,-5,0,5"
                        Text="{Binding Title}" />
                    </StackLayout>
                </Grid>
            </local:AccessoryViewCell>
        </DataTemplate>
        <templates:BreachOrPasteTemplateSelector x:Key="breachOr
        PasteTemplateSelector" BreachTemplate="{StaticResource
        breachCellTemplate}" PasteTemplate="{StaticResource
        pasteCellTemplate}" />
    </ResourceDictionary>
</ContentPage.Resources>
```

In the resources, you can see that two DataTemplates are defined—breachCellTemplate and pasteCellTemplate. And finally, there is the DataTemplateSelector. Since the DataTemplate is just a layout, let's focus on the BreachOrPasteTemplateSelector. You can see it has a key and properties for the two templates. In Listing 6-12, you can see the class.

Listing 6-12. Implementation of the DataTemplateSelector Class

```
public class BreachOrPasteTemplateSelector : DataTemplateSelector
{
    public DataTemplate BreachTemplate { get; set; }
    public DataTemplate PasteTemplate { get; set; }

    protected override DataTemplate OnSelectTemplate
    (object item, BindableObject container)
    {
        return item is Breach ? BreachTemplate : PasteTemplate;
    }
}
```

To implement a custom template selector class, it needs to inherit from the DataTemplateSelector class. The most important part is the OnSelectTemplate method override. Here you implement the logic that is used to determine which template should be used for the item that is coming in. The item will be the object that is in the collection behind the ListView and is evaluated. In my implementation in Listing 6-12, I check to see if item is of type Breach. If it is, I return one template, if not, I return the other. But you can build any kind of logic that you might want here. Also, I created two properties to supply the DataTemplates, and you could also choose to build these in code or some other way. I choose this way so I could define them in XAML.

Behaviors

There is one more thing to discover in the ListView code of Listing 6-10. You can see the Behaviors property. With a behavior, you can extend the functionality of a control, without having to create your own subclass. In this case, a behavior is used to enable a Command, whenever an item in the list is selected. Oddly enough, there is no support for it by default at the time of writing this book. Normally, you should bind to the SelectedItem property of the ListView to trigger logic whenever an item is selected.

But since you can only use a property for this, this is not ideal. The other option is to go with the ItemSelected event, but since it uses an event, this is not great to use with the MVVM pattern. So, basically, this behavior is converting the ItemSelected event into a command, which is a common use case with behaviors. There is much more to these behaviors and if you want to know more, check out: https://developer.xamarin. com/guides/xamarin-forms/application-fundamentals/behaviors/.

A thing that is commonly said about the ListView is that it does not perform very well depending on which properties you set to a certain value. Especially on the Android platform, performance can be poor when you enable properties that require computations, like setting the HasUnevenRows to true, which causes more measurement to take place. While the team at Xamarin is working hard to make it as performant as they can, have a look at what you can do yourself here: https:// developer.xamarin.com/guides/xamarin-forms/user-interface/ listview/performance/.

To read everything about the ListView, you can turn to the Xamarin pages at https://developer.xamarin.com/guides/xamarin-forms/user-interface/listview/.

Custom Views and Controls

The final notable elements on this page are the ones shown in Listing 6-13.

Listing 6-13. Custom Views

```
<views:LoadingView Grid.Row="1" Grid.RowSpan="2" IsVisible="
{Binding IsLoading}"/>
<views:ErrorView Grid.Row="1" Grid.RowSpan="2" IsVisible="
{Binding IsError}"/>
```

While these might look kind of odd at first, there isn't really that much to it actually. Basically, we took out a piece of XAML and put it in its own element. That way, the `MainPage.xaml` stays a bit cleaner and we can reuse this element easier in another page. You can see by their names— `LoadingView` and `ErrorView`—that these views are used when data is being loaded or when some error occurred.

To see the contents of the `LoadingView` as an example, check out `https://github.com/jfversluis/been-pwned/blob/master/src/BeenPwnedApp/Core/Views/LoadingView.xaml`. It doesn't add anything to show the contents here, as it is just an arbitrary view. The thing to take away here is that you can move this XAML into its own file to keep your pages tidy.

The way this concept works is that it lets these general loading or error views span the whole page and make sure that certain elements are shown or hidden by properties in the `PageModel`. You have to make sure that the right elements are shown and hidden at the right state of your application. Beware that doing it this way might affect the performance when you have more complex layouts, as the view might be rendered even when it's not visible.

The PageModel

Now that you have seen all of the page, what remains is the corresponding `PageModel`. I think the most relevant parts are already handled inline. But let's look at some of the global concepts of the `PageModel` when using FreshMvvm.

The first thing you need to know is that a `PageModel` has to be a subclass of the `FreshBasePageModel`. This class has a few methods that can be overridden. These methods are:

- **Init**: This method is called when this `PageModel` is pushed. It also has one parameter, `initData`, with which data can be transferred from the `PageModel` that pushed this one. For example, when you select an item from a list, you can supply the ID of whole object to show in a more detailed view.

- **ReverseInit**: This method is the opposite of Init. This method is called on the `PageModel` that pushed the new `PageModel`. The `ReverseInit` method also has one parameter, with which you can return a value to the calling PageModel.

- **ViewIsAppearing**: When a new page is pushed, this method will fire when the page is shown. If you paid attention to the MVVM pattern, you might find this a bit weird. There should be no relation whatsoever between the PageModel and the page. But FreshMvvm lets you access the page from the PageModel. While this is not in line with pure MVVM, it comes in handy sometimes. But beware—*you* are responsible for not creating strong dependencies between the page and the `PageModel`.

- **ViewIsDisappearing**: The opposite of ViewIsAppearing.

It might also be a good idea to create your own base `PageModel` class. You will probably have some properties that are shared among all your `PageModels`, like for instance a boolean to indicate that data is loading or an error occurred.

To look at the PageModel that belongs to the page that we looked at in this chapter in particular, visit `https://github.com/jfversluis/` `been-pwned/blob/master/src/BeenPwnedApp/Core/PageModels/` `MainPageModel.cs`.

Working with Resources and Metadata

In this chapter, you have seen several images in action. The use of images is something that is best handled per platform. Each platform has its own infrastructure to make sure that your images are optimized for different resolutions. In addition, more metadata has to be collected for your app, which is also handled differently per platform.

Let's take a moment to review how Apple and Google have implemented this in iOS and Android, respectively.

iOS

On iOS, working with images is pretty straightforward. There is a `Resources` folder in your iOS project in which you should put your resources, which are mostly images. At the time of writing this book, there are three resolution scales available across all iOS versions. However, the iOS versions that are currently supported by Apple only use two resolution scales.

If you want to support the oldest devices, you will just add an image with the smallest dimensions in pixels, and for instance you name it `MyIcon.png`. Now, if you want to support all resolutions, you will need to add the same icon twice and three times as big as the original one and name them `MyIcon@2x.png` and `MyIcon@3x.png`, respectively. The iOS operating system will automatically select the right version depending on what device and thus, what resolution, your app is running on.

In your Xamarin.Forms layout, you can just specify your `MyIcon.png` filename. Forms will then also select the right version for you, but you will still need to let the images reside in the platform's native resources folder.

For more information on the different image sizes needed for usage in various controls, refer to the Human Interface Guidelines at `https://developer.apple.com/ios/human-interface-guidelines/icons-and-images/image-size-and-resolution/`.

Besides working with images—or better resources—there is more metadata that needs to be set for the app. Think in the range of which devices are supported, which orientations are supported, what is the minimum iOS version, and much more. All these settings can be found in the `info.plist` file. The most important settings are done when you first set up your project, such as your app name and unique identifier—you know, the reverse domain.

Visual Studio on Windows and Mac both have a designer to configure this file. Just double-click the `info.plist` file to open it.

I won't go through all the settings; it should be pretty straightforward. If you need any help, refer to the Xamarin documentation at `https://developer.xamarin.com/guides/ios/application_fundamentals/working_with_property_lists/`.

You need to set some keys whenever you need permission to access a user's photos or location. You need to add a description stating the reason that you want access, so that the users can make informed decisions. Not setting these keys will result in a silent fail at runtime and, if this slipped your mind, you will find yourself searching, which is a waste on such a small detail. Incidentally, Apple adds such a property, so be aware.

Last, make sure that any resource you place in the iOS resources folder is marked with the `BundleResource` build action in Visual Studio.

Android

The Android platform takes a slightly different approach, although the outcome is the same. Instead of having to name the files individually, you need to place a file with the same name in a different folder. On Android, under the `Resources` folder there will be a subfolder for each screen resolution. The infrastructure is a bit more complex than on iOS, because there are a lot more variations in devices that run Android.

In a typical scenario, you would have a bunch of folders under your resources, such as `drawable-ldpi`, `drawable-hdpi`, `drawable-xhdpi`, etc. As you might have deduced from the names, the images are arrange by *dots per inch* (DPI). However, this is just one of the possibilities. You can also arrange them by localization, for instance. To read all about the resources on Android, refer to the Android documentation at `https://developer.android.com/guide/topics/resources/providing-resources.html`.

To have different resolutions for each version, you simply place a file with the same name in each subfolder that you want to support. So, let's say you have the same `MyIcon.png` file in different resolutions. You put each one, with the same name, in its respective folder.

Just like with iOS, Android will sort out the right image for the right device. In Xamarin.Forms, you just have to state the filename, and Forms will take care of the rest. Keep in mind that the Android platform does not accept hyphens in filenames. So, to keep everything in check, you might want to prevent using hyphens in iOS filenames as well. If you do include a hyphen, Android will throw you a very unclear exception.

On Android, you need to provide metadata for your app as well. It will have roughly the same options as the `info.plist` file on iOS. The options on Android can be found under the `Properties` folder, in the `AndroidManifest.xml` file under your Android project. Unlike iOS, no fancy editor will come up directly. You can, however, set some of the options in the project properties.

For all these options, refer to the Android documentation at `https://developer.android.com/guide/topics/manifest/manifest-intro.html`.

Tip   To save yourself a lot of time and effort resizing images, look at the MFractor plugin for Visual Studio, both on Mac and Windows. This tool has a lot of great features, and one of them is an image import tool that will resize images for you.

Summary

This is the chapter we have been building up to. This chapter discussed a lot of different elements and I can imagine it is a bit much to take in all at once. You learned about the lifecycle methods in the `App.xaml.cs` file, which you can use to trigger logic whenever the app is started or sent to the background.

Furthermore, the chapter picked apart the `MainPage.xaml` and its `PageModel`, `MainPageModel.cs`, and it looked at the most common elements in Xamarin.Forms. It covered the things you should be wary of when using them.

The next chapter covers how to communicate with a backend. The data in the app has to come from somewhere and there are good methods to retrieve it.

CHAPTER 7

Connecting to a REST Backend

Now that you have seen how the app works in an architectural sense and learned how to build screens, it is time to retrieve some actual data.

I don't have any numbers or study to back this up, but I dare to make the claim that the percentage of apps that retrieve or send some kind of data to or from a backend service is very close to a hundred.

This chapter looks at various ways to communicate with the backend. It focuses on REST (Representational State Transfer) backends, which are popular because they use common HTTP for communication principles. In the first part, I show you how to make requests to an API backend manually. By this, I mean writing the full code for each request.

From there, we look at the Refit library. This library helps you write less repetitive code when creating requests to a backend by generating the code for you.

In the last part of this chapter, you learn about using third-party libraries that take care of the communication for you. This is the way the "been pwned" app was implemented.

Since this book focuses on the Xamarin.Forms app, I assume that you have some basic knowledge on REST API backends and how they work in general. If you do not, I recommend reading background information about REST APIs, idempotence, and the working of HTTP and HTTP verbs.

© Gerald Versluis 2017
G. Versluis, *Xamarin.Forms Essentials*, https://doi.org/10.1007/978-1-4842-3240-8_7

The Manual Way

To get the best understanding of how stuff in general works, I like to start off manually. This way, you will learn the most. Also, when you start looking at other libraries to take some repetitive code out of your hands, you will know what happens in the library and understand any errors you encounter. It will also help you appreciate the library and the authors if you know what they do for you.

As mentioned earlier, I like to name classes that provide data services, and it will be no surprise that I put them in the Services folder of the shared project. Because I use a third-party library for the "been pwned" app, code in this example won't be found in the actual project.

The first thing you need to do is identify all the endpoints that you want to communicate with. If you wrote the backend yourself, the endpoints should be familiar. If someone else provided the backend, there is probably some documentation for it somewhere that identifies the endpoints. The most common ones will use the GET and POST HTTP verbs to retrieve and send data, respectively. The documentation of the haveibeenpwned.com API can be found at https://haveibeenpwned.com/API/. Because most calls will roughly look the same, I walk you through one or two. The basic layout of my service class can be seen in Listing 7-1.

Listing 7-1. Outline of the Class That Will Act As a Service to Get Data from the haveibeenpwned.com API

```
public class BeenPwnedService
{
        public BeenPwnedService()
        {
        // TODO
        }
```

```
public async Task<IEnumerable<object>> GetBreaches()
{
// TODO
}

public async Task PostBreach(object breach)
{
  // TODO
}
}
```

There is nothing very complicated about it. There will be a constructor to instantiate the *HttpClient*, which will handle the communication. Furthermore, I show you two methods to retrieve data and send data. Note that there is no endpoint on the HIBP API that accepts POST requests, so I make one up for this. The actual code for this will not work.

First let's see how to set up the HttpClient. In the class, I've created a private field to hold the client. It is very likely that there will be multiple calls toward the API, so to avoid any overhead on creating the client for every request, the class will keep an instance for us. Look at Listing 7-2 for the private field and the implementation of the constructor code.

Listing 7-2. Implementation of the HttpClient

```
private readonly HttpClient _httpClient;

public BeenPwnedService()
{
    _httpClient = new HttpClient
    {
        BaseAddress = new Uri("https://haveibeenpwned.com/
        api/v2/")
    };
```

```
_httpClient.DefaultRequestHeaders.UserAgent.Clear();
_httpClient.DefaultRequestHeaders.UserAgent.Add
(new ProductInfoHeaderValue("Test", "1"));
}
```

In the constructor of this service, there is code to create a new instance of the HttpClient. We provide this client with the BaseAddress property. This address is used for every request that is made through the client. At the end, you can see it says v2. This is to identify that we are using version 2 of the API endpoints. This is known as *versioning*. The idea is that whenever you release a final version of an endpoint at the API side, you freeze that code—or better—you freeze the *contract*.

To communicate with a certain endpoint, you need to send a request that is understood by the API and it will send you a response in a certain format in return. This is the contract. Whenever something is about to change in either the parameters that you need to send with the request or in the data you can receive back, it is a good practice to create a new version. This way, old applications that call upon the v2 endpoint keep working and have time to switch over to the new version.

As you can see, there are two more lines. These are needed to identify the app to the HIBP API. Troy Hunt implemented this as a way of logging and security, probably. The API must send a user-agent identifier with each request. Failing to do so will result in an error.

This is a very simple form of security, but you can imagine that almost every API has some form limiting access. There can be many variations on this, so it's impossible to describe all of them. Most of them require you to provide some kind of token or other credential with each request; in this case, it's the user-agent HTTP header.

Now that the HttpClient is ready to send requests, let's see how to do this. Listing 7-3 implements the call to retrieve all breaches from the system.

Listing 7-3. Implementation of the Get Breaches Method

```
public async Task<IEnumerable<object>> GetBreaches()
{
    var response = await _httpClient.GetStringAsync("breaches");

    return JsonConvert.DeserializeObject<IEnumerable<object>>
    (response);
}
```

First, we simply retrieve the string contents of the API response. By simply calling the _httpClient.GetStringAsync("breaches") line, we will invoke a GET request to https://haveibeenpwned.com/api/v2/ breaches. Because we gave the HttpClient a base address already, we now only need to specify the endpoint, which is breaches.

The result of this call will be all breaches in the HIBP database in JavaScript Object Notation (*JSON*) format. JSON is a very popular format to describe data structures. It is similar to XML, but much more lightweight. A sample of the HIBP JSON response object is shown in Listing 7-4.

Listing 7-4. Sample JSON Response from the HIBP API, Showing One Record

```
[{"Title":"000webhost","Name":"000webhost","Domain":"000webh
ost.com","BreachDate":"2015-03-01","AddedDate":"2015-10-26T23
:35:45Z","ModifiedDate":"2015-10-26T23:35:45Z","PwnCount":1354
5468,"Description":"In approximately March 2015, the free web
hosting provider <a href=\"http://www.troyhunt.com/2015/10/
breaches-traders-plain-text-passwords.html\" target=\"_blank\"
rel=\"noopener\">000webhost suffered a major data breach</a>
that exposed over 13 million customer records. The data was sold
and traded before 000webhost was alerted in October. The breach
included names, email addresses and plain text passwords.","DataCl
```

asses":["Email addresses","IP addresses","Names","Passwords"],"Is Verified":true,"IsFabricated":false,"IsSensitive":false,"IsActive":true,"IsRetired":false,"IsSpamList":false,"LogoType":"png"}]

This JSON object shows a collection of breach records, showing one record for this example. A *collection* is denoted by the *square brackets*. One *object instance* is indicated by the *curly brackets*. Inside the curly brackets, you can then basically see key-value pairs, separated by a colon. The string before the colon is the name of the property and the value after the colon is the value of that property. The type of the property is inferred by its value. For example, the Title property has a value surrounded by quotes, so that is a string. When we look at the AddedDate, we also see a string, but this will be parsed as a DateTime because of its value. And later on, there is also the IsVerified property, which has a boolean value.

A property in itself can also have a collection and/or object. This way, you can transfer complex objects to a string and then serialize and deserialize them. There is a very good library for this, namely Json.NET. This library is used in the second line of the GET method in Listing 7-3. With this library, we deserialize the retrieved JSON content and return it as a string of objects. In real code, we would've implemented a model that holds all the properties for us; for now, I just deserialize it to a generic object. More on the Json.NET library in Chapter 8.

The final method of our service is shown in Listing 7-5.

Listing 7-5. Implementation of the Post Request to the API

```
public async Task PostBreach(object breach)
{
    var jsonObject = JsonConvert.SerializeObject(breach);

    await _httpClient.PostAsync("breaches",
        new StringContent(jsonObject, Encoding.UTF8,
        "application/json"));
}
```

As I mentioned, this endpoint is made up by me, so this will not actually work since the HIBP API does not provide any POST endpoints. But let's pretend there is such an endpoint and that it lets us send a breach object back to the API, which is then saved in the database. What we see happening is actually the exact way around as with the GET method. We now take in the breach object, serialize it into a JSON string, and then send it to the API using the line await _httpClient.PostAsync("breaches", new StringContent(jsonObject, Encoding.UTF8, "application/json")); line.

You see how the word GET was replaced with POST in the method that we call. Yet the endpoint name is still breaches. This works because now we do not call the endpoint with the GET verb, but with the POST verb. That is one way to distinguish between different operations on the same endpoint. Another way is to just name them different. But the most common way is to group your endpoints by a certain operation or entity and then use GET to retrieve one or more of those objects, POST to insert one, PUT to update, etc. There are various ways to solve these problems for all kinds of different requirements.

Because we posted something now, we need to send some content for the API to save. We will send the serialized object as a StringContent object. With this object, we can specify the encoding of the string and, just as important, the *media-type,* also known as the Multipurpose Internet Mail Extensions (MIME) type. The MIME type specifies what type of content the string holds. This can for instance be text/html to indicate that the string holds HTML content. For JSON, this is application/json. To learn more about different types, look at the Wikipedia page at https://en.wikipedia.org/wiki/Media_type.

If this code was to be used in a real-life scenario, there are some improvements that would need to be made, so don't just copy and paste it. Try to understand what it does. That way, you can improve the code and keep it performant and secure. Improvements you could try include error handling to see if a request succeeded, disposing the HttpClient to free up memory, and more.

The Refit Way

In the previous part of this chapter, you saw how to implement calls to the backend. While this works perfectly, a lot of code will be repeated. We have to (de)serialize the object every time and send it through a GET or POST method. If there is one thing we do not like as developers, it's repeated code. A package that can help you with this is Refit, by Paul Betts.

By using this library, you can omit all the implantation code, as it will be generated at compile-time by Refit. The only thing you have to do is define an interface with the signatures of the endpoints that you want to communicate with. Then all these methods will be adorned with attributes to specify some metadata, like if the call is a POST of a GET and what the URL is. Let's look at how this works if we wanted to transform our manual class from the previous part into a Refit solution.

Start by installing the Refit NuGet package into the shared project and also the platform projects. We can then simply define an interface like in Listing 7-6.

Listing 7-6. Interface for Our API Calls

```
[Headers("Accent: application/json")]
public interface IBeenPwnedService
{
    [Get("/breaches")]
    Task<IEnumerable<object>> GetBreaches();

    [Post("/breaches")]
    Task PostBreach(object breach);
}
```

If you look closely, you will notice that I used the method names from our initial class in the previous part of this chapter. But now, we only have to declare these method signatures. By putting the GET and POST attributes above them, Refit will figure out if it should be a GET or POST request. As a parameter to these attributes, we provide the endpoint name. There is also a Headers attribute above the interface definition. That way, you can send headers with each request that is made. You can also move the Header attribute to one method; it will only be sent with that one method.

Note that all methods must return a Task, since they will be implemented asynchronously. Also, make sure that the endpoints start with a forward slash, or it will result in a runtime error.

For all options that are available—and there are quite a lot—you can check out the projects GitHub page at https://github.com/paulcbetts/refit. One that I would like to mention is how to incorporate dynamic parameters directly into your endpoint URL. It is not uncommon to retrieve a certain object by its ID. An endpoint could then look like this: https://haveibeenpwned.com/api/v2/breachedaccount/my-username. Because we now define the endpoints with an attribute, we cannot simply add values to it. This has been accounted for in Refit. When you define the endpoint in the attribute like this:

```
[Post("/breachedaccount/{account}")]
Task<object> GetBreachesForAccount(string account);
```

It will automatically insert the value of the account parameter into the endpoint by matching the parameter name; no code required. Pretty awesome, right?

Since we can't call on an interface directly and we do need a little bit of configuration, we do need some sort of client to execute these requests. This client can be seen in Listing 7-7.

Listing 7-7. Implementation of the New Service Class

```
public class BeenPwnedService
{
    private readonly IBeenPwnedService _beenpwnedClient;

    public BeenPwnedService()
    {
        var httpClient = new HttpClient
        {
            BaseAddress = new Uri("https://haveibeenpwned.com/
            api/v2/")
        };

        _beenpwnedClient = RestService.For<IBeenPwnedService>(h
        ttpClient);
    }

    public async Task<IEnumerable<object>> GetBreaches()
    {
        return await _beenpwnedClient.GetBreaches();
    }

    public async Task PostBreach(object breach)
    {
        await _beenpwnedClient.PostBreach(breach);
    }
}
```

The only thing that remains of the original are some wrapper methods around the interface. To let Refit generate a class for you, you can simply call RestService.For<IBeenPwnedService>(httpClient) ;. You can see that we still need to provide for the HttpClient. This is actually to our advantage, as we could choose another transportation stack if we wanted to.

In earlier versions of Xamarin.Forms, the `HttpClient` implementation of .NET was used. While this supported the most features, it was not the fastest option. Back then, you had to implement your own message handler to leverage the native HTTP stacks on iOS and Android, which were much faster. This is the default setting in Xamarin.Forms. Normally, you would not have to worry about this. Because we set the `HttpClient` here, you could also implement your required security headers in here.

Then, as you can see, we simply pass along the interface methods calls through here. If you wanted to, you could do some translation or other logic like error handling before you send it back to your business logic.

Now you can just instantiate the `BeenPwnedService` class as you did before and call on it. This saves a lot of repetitive code! It's good to know that when `Refit` receives an HTTP response that's not an OK status code, it will throw an exception. So you need to account for that.

The Third-Party Way

When you didn't build the backend you're communicating with, chances are good that the author or another third-party author developed a library. This is sort of true for communication with `haveibeenpwned.com`. There is a library available for it, but I wrote it myself in anticipation of rebuilding the "been pwned" app. This way, other developers might find it easier to incorporate functionality in their applications as well. For the sake of this example, we will treat this library as if it were built by someone else and we want to use it in our app.

To find a library, you can either look at the associated web site or search for it on Google, GitHub, or NuGet. Whenever you find one that suits your needs, you can install it into your app through NuGet. Chances are good that the library is open-source and the source is available online for you to see. (Or at least there should be some documentation on how to get started.) The code for the `BeenPwned.Api` library can be found on GitHub at `https://github.com/jfversluis/BeenPwned.Api/`. To install it, simply find it on NuGet.

After installation, you simply create the service class again and call the methods in the installed third-party library.

The example in the "been pwned" app can be seen in Listing 7-8. This example has been simplified a bit from the actual code at `https://github.com/jfversluis/been-pwned/blob/master/src/BeenPwnedApp/Core/Services/BeenPwnedService.cs` because the production version implements some error handling and caching.

Listing 7-8. Implementation of the Third-Party Communication Service

```
public class BeenPwnedService
{
    private IBeenPwnedClient _pwnedClient = new
    BeenPwnedClient($"BeenPwned-{Device.RuntimePlatform}");

    public IObservable<IEnumerable<Breach>> GetAllBreaches(bool
    force = false)
    {
        return await _pwnedClient.GetAllBreaches();
    }

    public async Task<IEnumerable<Breach>>
    GetBreachesForAccount(string account, string domain = "",
    bool includeUnverified = false)
    {
        return await _pwnedClient.GetBreachesForAccount
        (account, domain, false, includeUnverified);
    }

    public async Task<bool> GetIsPasswordPwned(string password)
    {
        return await _pwnedClient.GetPwnedPassword(password);
    }
```

```
public async Task<IEnumerable<Paste>> GetPastesFor
Account(string account)
{
    return await _pwnedClient.GetPastesForAccount(account);
}
}
```

In the private field, you see how a new client is instantiated with a parameter that will be used as the user-agent header. All the code for the endpoints, setting the user-agent, and using the HttpClient is now abstracted into the NuGet package.

The rest of the calls are calling on the third-party library and wrapping it in our own logic where needed.

Summary

There are of course more ways to connect to a backend than are described in this chapter. For one, not all services will be REST (although most modern backends will likely be). One question that I hear sometimes is how to connect to a PHP or Node.js backend. If those services work the REST way and communicate through the HTTP protocol, there is no reason that the code in this chapter will not work. In fact, I don't even know in what language and what technique the haveibeenpwned.com API is built, and I don't have to!

This chapter showed you how to communicate with a backend service, based on the REST principles. It showed you how to implement all the calls by hand, so you will have a better understanding of how the communication works in detail.

From there, we looked at how the Refit library can help you reduce the amount of code needed for communication. This helps you achieve better maintainability and just to have more time for coffee. I didn't even mention this yet, but the great thing is that Refit can be used in other projects than just Xamarin apps! You can use it in most of your .NET-based projects.

Finally, you learned how to work with a third-party library. This is the simplest way of connecting to a backend. You typically drop in the library and call the right methods.

This chapter concludes most of the actual development. With everything you have learned up until now, you should be able to build a Xamarin.Forms app that gets data from an external source. Of course, there are more challenges to overcome, but you're well on your way.

The next chapter looks at other libraries, just as awesome as Refit, that are used in most of my apps. By studying these libraries, you will know what is out there, so you don't have to reinvent the wheel. This will help clarify some of the more important concepts of mobile development.

CHAPTER 8

Using Good Libraries That Are Already Out There

Throughout this book I have mentioned that there are a lot of good libraries out there. Some of them I have mentioned by name, others I didn't mention at all. This chapter lists a couple of libraries that come in very handy in various scenarios.

For each library, I will give you a brief overview of what it does and provide links to the project web site.

I once more want to emphasize that installing a NuGet often means that you have to install it on the shared project *and* the platform project. While I am writing this book, we are also in the transition from PCL libraries to .NET Standard libraries. There are some libraries that do not support .NET Standard yet or the other way around; they have dropped support for PCLs already. Be sure to check your requirements before you get yourself into trouble halfway there.

To overcome the dropped support of the .NET Standard library, you could install an older version of the NuGet. However, realize that you are not working with the latest version and it could contain bugs or not have implemented the latest features. Use it as a last resort.

FreshMvvm

I have mentioned this library a couple of times. This is my favorite MVVM framework for Xamarin.Forms to date. This framework by Michael Ridland is very lightweight and adds just the right number of missing features. With the built-in IoC container, setting up dependency injection is a breeze.

Since I have already written a lot about implementing FreshMvvm, I won't go over it again here, but be sure to check it out. There are many more possibilities than the things I have shown you.

The project can be found on GitHub at https://github.com/rid00z/FreshMvvm.

Refit

Another library I mentioned in the previous chapter is Refit by Paul Betts. This library is super handy for getting rid of all the repeated code you have to write for communicating with your REST API backend. By simply defining the outline of your API in an interface, the rest of the code is generated for you!

The features I have shown you in Chapter 7 just start to scratch the surface. This is enough to get you started, but don't be fooled into thinking that is all. If you want more advanced scenarios, it's all supported. I have yet to find a missing feature and I have built an app or two with this.

The source code and documentation for this project can be found at https://github.com/paulcbetts/refit.

Polly

One library that I didn't mention yet is Polly. This library takes error handling to the next level. Things like retry mechanisms with incremented intervals, defining policies, circuit breaking, fallbacks, and timeouts are all in here. All of this goodness is very easy to implement with the fluent syntax.

This kind of functionality comes in rather handy if you're working with connections that aren't always stable, like with mobile devices. You might want to retry a request a couple of times before handing the error to your user.

Especially when used together with other smart mechanisms like Akavache, which you will see next, this can be a very powerful library to provide a good user experience, even when things start to go bad.

The project can be found on GitHub at `https://github.com/App-vNext/Polly`.

Akavache

This library is all about caching and storing key-value data. The most I've used it for is caching. You can very easily implement this library in your services in the app, to provide the user with cached data while fetching live data in the background. That way, the user is never presented with an empty screen, which provides for a better user experience.

We use this library in the HIBP app. You can see the full code at `https://github.com/jfversluis/been-pwned/blob/master/src/BeenPwnedApp/Core/Services/BeenPwnedService.cs`, but I also provide the relevant snippet in Listing 8-1.

Listing 8-1. Sample Implementation of Working with Akavache

```
internal IObservable<IEnumerable<Breach>> GetAllBreaches(bool
force = false)
{
        var cache = BlobCache.LocalMachine;
    return cache.GetAndFetchLatest("breaches", async () =>
    await _pwnedClient.GetAllBreaches(),
        offset =>
        {
```

```
        //If there is no network connection available,
        always return false so that the user will get
        cached data if available
        if (CrossConnectivity.Current.IsConnected)
        {
            TimeSpan elapsed = DateTimeOffset.Now - offset;
            var invalidate = (force || elapsed > new
            TimeSpan(24, 0, 0));
            return invalidate;
        }
        else
            return false;
    });
}
```

This method retrieves all the breaches in the system. We use the GetAndFetchLatest method to call on the cache store. This method takes three parameters. The first is a string, which specifies the key to store the retrieved values. Second is the method that will be used to retrieve the actual data. Lastly, there is the method to determine whether new data is to be fetched. You can implement logic to determine if your data is still relevant, or if it has to be invalidated. It's as easy as that!

By returning the IObservable type, we can hook into the callback on our PageModel and update the data whenever it comes in. This way, the user gets it without probably even noticing.

Details for all of this can be found at https://github.com/akavache/Akavache.

Fusillade

Another library by Paul Betts is Fusillade. He calls it "an opinionated HTTP library for mobile development".

You can use this library to optimize your calls to the backend. Basically, it provides a set of `HttpMessageHandlers` that makes handling web requests more efficient and therefore more responsive.

The things `Fusillade` can do for you include:

- *Automatic deduplication of requests*: Imagine that you're building a social media app and each item in the list can have the same avatar and username of certain users. `Fusillade` will detect the same request to that avatar and execute it only once, saving a lot of unnecessary requests.

- *Limiting requests*: Requests are limited to four at a time by default. This limits the pressure on the—sometimes limited—network connection.

- *Prioritizing requests*: You can implement some mechanics to let `Fusillade` know if a load has been initiated from the background or by a user. In the latter case, the request will be rendered more important and is prioritized over others.

- *Speculative requests*: You can implement a pre-load mechanism for certain requests that you expect the user to click on so it will load faster, simply because it is already loaded. You can specify the amount of maximum content to be pre-loaded.

So, all in all, pretty powerful stuff. It can be somewhat tricky to implement, but it can also help you get that last bit of optimization.

This project is found on GitHub at `https://github.com/paulcbetts/Fusillade`.

Settings

There are quite a few libraries by James Montemagno, a former Xamarin, now Microsoft, employee. The whole list of plugins he has been writing or contributing to can be found at https://github.com/jamesmontemagno/Xamarin.Plugins.

Xam.Plugins.Settings is one of them. As you might have guessed, this plugin is all about settings. It can be used to store all kinds of application settings for your users. You can also do this by using Application.Current.Properties and leveraging the .NET configuration engine, but this plugin uses the native way for each platform.

When you install it, you will be presented with a helper class that has some boilerplate code, as shown in Listing 8-2.

Listing 8-2. Helper Class As Provided by the Settings Plugin

```
public static class Settings
{
    private static ISettings AppSettings
    {
        get
        {
            return CrossSettings.Current;
        }
    }

    #region Setting Constants

    private const string SettingsKey = "settings_key";
    private static readonly string SettingsDefault = string.
    Empty;
```

```
#endregion

public static string GeneralSettings
{
    get
    {
        return AppSettings.GetValueOrDefault(SettingsKey,
        SettingsDefault);
    }

    set
    {
        AppSettings.AddOrUpdateValue(SettingsKey, value);
    }
}
}
```

You can see that this is very easy to extend. Just add a new property for each setting that you want and, by simply setting a value, it is directly saved. You can also bind directly to the properties in this class from your user interface to have the users configure their settings.

Note that only simple types are supported.

This project is hosted on GitHub at `https://github.com/` `jamesmontemagno/SettingsPlugin`.

Connectivity

Seeing that we have talked about the network connection on a mobile device a couple of times now, it seems that is important. And it is! That's why I did not want to keep this plugin from you. It's called `Xam.Plugin.` `Connectivity`, also by James Montemagno.

With this library, you can check whether you have a connection and if you can reach certain hosts. It also allows you to hook into the event of the connection status changing. Before, I talked about how to handle failed requests and recover. With this connectivity library, you can check beforehand if a connection is available and working and inform your users proactively.

You have seen it in action in Listing 8-1. There is a line that reads: `CrossConnectivity.Current.IsConnected`. With this simple line, you can determine if the device is connected. If it's not, the code doesn't even bother trying the request. This is also very helpful when you're updating your UI, by informing your user to check their connection.

The source and documentation for this library can be found at `https://github.com/jamesmontemagno/ConnectivityPlugin`.

PropertyChanged.Fody

Just like with `Refit`, implementing the `INotifyPropertyChanged` interface will create a lot of similar code in your project as well. You saw this in Chapter 5.

To be able to omit a lot of this code and make it more readable, you can use the `PropertyChanged.Fody` library. You drop in this library and have your classes implement the `INotifyPropertyChanged` interface. The code for triggering the UI update is generated automatically at runtime for your properties with a setter. There are also a lot of attributes available that you can use on your properties to influence the generated code. For instance, you can use the `AlsoNotifyFor` attribute to trigger the update for another property that needs to be updated in conjunction with the first one.

You can read all about this project at `https://github.com/Fody/PropertyChanged`.

FFImageLoading

Loading, showing, and transforming images can be a difficult task. With FFImageLoading (Fast & Furious Image Loading), working with images is easy.

This library is capable of a lot. At the very core, it can be used to cache images. Downloading images from the web can involve expensive calls. By caching these images, you can cut back on loading times and data usage of your app. Another thing that is not uncommon when working with images is excessive memory usage. When you squeeze in images that are too big, your app will eat up the memory and become unusable. With FFImageLoading, you can downsample your images to the right size, and it will not use excessive memory.

Usage is easy; you just install the library—remember: on all your projects—and use the CachedImage element instead of the normal Image element. And that is it for the basic usage. On the CachedImage element, you now have a lot of properties at hand to optimize viewing your pictures. On top of that, you also get placeholders for when the image is loading or when an error occurs while loading and much more.

You can also install the separate Transformations package. With this package, you can apply all kinds of transformations to your image. Think of transformations like blurring, creating a circular image, or converting an image to grayscale. You can even add your own transformation if it isn't supplied by default. It is used in the "been pwned" app as well, as it supports SVG images.

The GitHub repository for this library can be found at https:// github.com/luberda-molinet/FFImageLoading.

UserDialogs

In Forms, you can only spawn a dialog directly from a page. This is a problem, because we want all our logic to happen in the `PageModel`. That is where `UserDialogs`, by Allan Ritchie, comes in. With the `UserDialogs` plugin, you can create dialogs with a static class from anywhere in your code. It doesn't stop there. It also provides you with confirmation boxes, toasts, and other kinds of dialogs that aren't supported by Xamarin.Forms directly.

Actually, there isn't much more to say about it. It just works!

Find the GitHub at `https://github.com/aritchie/userdialogs`.

FormsCommunityToolkit

I have talked a bit about effects, converters, and behaviors. These can be used for accessing native properties, converting data binding values, and applying logic to elements, respectively. While custom implementations of these concepts are very easy to do, it's not recommended to duplicate it into all of your projects.

The `FormsCommunityToolkit` tries to unify some of the most implemented effects, converters, and behaviors.

For example, in this package you can find effects to remove the border on an `Entry` or disable the autocorrect functionality. These are things that aren't supported by Xamarin.Forms out of the box. If you want custom colors on your `Switch` control, this is the library for you.

There are behaviors for validating an e-mail address or numeric values and turning events into commands. Or what about the hex-to-color converter, or maybe you want your text to be converted to uppercase letters. All of these features are included in this package for you to use, and much, much more. If there is anything you're missing, the developers gladly accept pull requests for anything.

I have contributed a thing or two to this library, so I would be happy to know if you like it!

This toolkit can be found on GitHub at `https://github.com/ FormsCommunityToolkit/FormsCommunityToolkit`.

Other Tooling

Besides all the libraries that are out there, there is also tooling that allows you to be more productive. The following subsections describe some of the tooling options that is available.

MFractor

This one I mentioned earlier; it's `MFractor` by Matthew Robbins. This tool helps you fill the gaps that IntelliSense sometimes leaves when working with Xamarin and especially with XAML. It will notice missing properties in your `PageModels` or detect that it is of the wrong type and generate a converter for you.

Where it *really* helps is with the import wizard for images. It resizes images to the right dimensions and names them appropriately for all the different platforms. It is such a wonderful tool!

It has a free version, which is great, but to support Matthew, I suggest getting the paid version. It is money well spent. He is not paying me to say this, I swear!

As I am writing this book, only a Mac version is available for Visual Studio for Mac, but I know they are working hard to support Windows as well. By the time you are reading this, it may already be released. For the latest information, visit `https://www.mfractor.com/`.

Third-Party XAML Previewers

Nowadays, Xamarin.Forms has a XAML previewer incorporated in Visual Studio. It isn't perfect yet, but it helps a lot. While the default previewer was absent, some people have taken it upon themselves to create their own. They all offer mostly the same functionality, so there is no point in describing them all in detail. These previewers can save you some time! Instead of having to move an element pixel-by-pixel or change just a shade of that one color and then rebuild and run your whole app just to see it's still not right, you can now see changes happening live.

The two most notable XAML preview tools are these:

- *Gorilla Player*: `http://gorillaplayer.com/`

- *LiveXAML*: `http://www.livexaml.com/`

Xamarin Live Player

Another great "tool" is the recently introduced Xamarin Live Player by the team at Xamarin. You install this app on your physical device from the app store. Then you can see a preview of your app, right on your phone while you're working on it.

You start your project, scan a QR code with your phone. From that point on, every change you make is instantly available on your phone to review. This makes debugging on a physical device a whole lot easier. At the time of writing this book, the tool is in preview.

Everything about the Xamarin Live Player can be found at `https://www.xamarin.com/live`.

Summary

There is a very active and awesome community for Xamarin and Xamarin. Forms. Because of these smart and driven people, there is a lot of content already out there for you to use. If you need a custom control or need to access native device functionality, see if someone else has created a solution first. Chances are that there is already someone who has created something for you, ready to use. If you miss anything, they are open for suggestion and participation on their open-source projects.

This chapter showed you a handful of great libraries that I use in my almost every project. But this is just the tip of the iceberg. I hope you found it useful to get a glimpse and are eager to implement these into your own apps. Note that not all of these libraries are specific to Xamarin. You can use them in your other .NET applications as well.

In the next chapter, we look into the future. I describe in some detail what is to be expected of the next major version of Xamarin. Maybe the new version will already be out by the time you are reading this. If so, you can treat them as features you can use *today!*

PART III

Future of Xamarin.Forms

CHAPTER 9

What to Expect in Xamarin.Forms Version 3

As I was writing this book, the next major release of Xamarin.Forms, namely version 3, was looming. By the time you are reading this, version 3 will have probably made it to production. That means that some of the features I describe here are probably available to you right now.

Other features might be pushed back or dropped. Xamarin has communicated the features covered in this chapter, so chances of them being dropped aren't great. But still, be aware that this is all in the future as I write, so no guarantees!

You can see the full roadmap on the Xamarin Forums at `https://forums.xamarin.com/discussion/85747/xamarin-forms-feature-roadmap/p1.`

Improving Performance

The focus of version 3 of Xamarin.Forms is performance and stability. The team at Xamarin has learned a lot and has a few tricks up their sleeves to improve things here and there.

© Gerald Versluis 2017
G. Versluis, *Xamarin.Forms Essentials*, https://doi.org/10.1007/978-1-4842-3240-8_9

Fast Renderers

As you learned in Chapter 2, Xamarin uses platform renderers to achieve the translation from abstract controls to native ones. This is where most of the heavy lifting is done, so they are looking at where they can identify bottlenecks and remove them.

Especially on Android, performance can be problematic. For this, the Xamarin.Forms team is creating special *fast renderers*. These special renderers will reduce inflation—a concept used on Android to construct controls—and cut back on rendering time by flattening the nesting of controls.

The best thing about these renderers is that you do not have to do anything special to use them! Over time the "old" renderers will be replaced by the fast renderers, one by one. The first tests report up to two times faster rendering.

The `ListView` is always under heavy fire because it can hold an unlimited number of rows and can become slow, very quickly. With the new optimizations for this in place, scrolling should be a lot smoother with these new renderers.

Of course, all of this is still subject to the hardware, OS, and other factors that are being used.

Layout Compression

Xamarin.Forms is all about the elements and layouts, so logically, that is where we can still gain a lot on performance. One thing that helps already is enabling XAML compilation, as discussed in Chapter 6.

Layout compression is an addition to this. Not very much is known at this point about this feature, but it's said that when this is enabled, layouts will be optimized at compile time. This will improve render times and lower memory usage.

The way the Xamarin.Forms team wants to achieve this is by compressing multiple layers of Xamarin.Forms layouts into a single native view.

XAML Standard

Chapter 2 covered XAML in the WPF context. You learned that the naming is inconsistent between Xamarin.Forms and WPF (and UWP apps, for that matter). Now that everything XAML-based is back at Microsoft, efforts have been made to unify all the dialects. This is called the *XAML Standard*.

This means that, when a platform implements a certain version of the XAML Standard, you can use that XAML everywhere else that supports the same version. Basically, this is just like how .NET Standard works. In the future, this will mean you can write the same XAML for your Xamarin apps, WPF apps, UWP apps, and who knows what more is to come! Although I still think you should look at your layouts critically when porting from one form factor to another, this will be a big asset when porting.

You can read more, and even participate, on the specification on GitHub at `https://github.com/Microsoft/xaml-standard`.

More Styling Options

I believe this feature has moved back to the backlog for now, but at least it is still on there. Xamarin is looking into a more CSS-like styling syntax to be integrated into Xamarin.Forms. Not much is known about this feature, especially since it is being pushed back, but it sounds very promising! It would be great to have some of the great stuff that is available in CSS today, right in Xamarin.Forms. This will allow us to implement styling easier and maybe even theming capabilities for our apps.

Technically not styling, but it's right there on the same shelf is the introduction of the *FlexLayout* system. This is a very popular engine in the web development world. If you aren't really into web development; the FlexLayout system provides a way to efficiently lay out, distribute, and align space among items in a container. This also works for elements with an unknown size, hence the word "flex".

Read more about the use and workings of FlexLayout at `https://www.w3.org/TR/css-flexbox-1/`.

Xamarin.Forms Embedding

As you have seen earlier in this book, there is a simple way to use native controls directly in Xamarin.Forms, called *native embedding*. Now, the folks at Xamarin are introducing the opposite, called *Xamarin.Forms Embedding*. You can now also incorporate Xamarin.Forms controls into your traditional Xamarin apps!

This allows for all kinds of scenarios. Maybe you want to turn your traditional Xamarin app info a Xamarin.Forms one, but you don't have the resources to do it all at once. With Xamarin.Forms Embedding, you can do it gradually. Or maybe you just like that one control that Form has to offer; now you can use it.

Also, all other Xamarin.Forms goodies—like `DependencyService`, `MessagingCenter`, data binding, etc.—will work as well.

More Supported Platforms

With the basics now implemented, it is time to spread out across more platforms. The usual suspects are covered—iOS, Android, and UWP—and now they are moving on to MacOS and GTK#.

GTK# is a .NET wrapper for GTK+, a UI toolkit mainly used on Linux systems. This means that you can bring your Xamarin.Forms app to a variety of Linux distributions in the near future.

Did you know that you can already run Xamarin (Note: not Forms!) on platforms like PlayStation 4, Xbox, Google Glass, Amazon Kindle, and Linux?

Others

There is a lot more to come in this next version and the ones after that. To name a few—:globalization support, accessibility improvements, more gesture recognizers, and full support for .NET Standard 2.0. I could go on for a while.

The reason I don't describe these in more detail is simply because there isn't more detail available right now, but it seems that Microsoft has great plans for Xamarin and they seem to focus heavily on Xamarin.Forms specifically.

One more good thing to note is that support for Windows Phone 8 and 8.1 is being dropped as soon as possible. This platform isn't maintained by Microsoft anymore and removing support for Windows Phone from Xamarin.Forms should improve the startup times for apps built with Forms.

Summary

It looks like Microsoft is investing heavily on the development of Xamarin and especially of Forms. If you don't have any experience with it right now, I hope this book will inspire you to look at this great ecosystem and everything it has to offer.

This chapter peeked into the future of Xamarin.Forms and highlighted a couple key features that will be part of the upcoming major version of Forms.

CHAPTER 10

Conclusion

And it's a wrap! I hope you have enjoyed reading this book as much as I have enjoyed writing it. But before I leave you to start awesome projects on your own, I'd like to point out some other resources you can check out.

Besides writing books, I also have a blog, which covers basic things, but also not-so basic things. You can check it out at `https://blog.verslu.is/`. And while I was writing blogs and the example code that comes with them, I thought to myself, "Why not start a screen recording while I am creating the sample code?". So I got into some vlogging as well. These videos are actually in line with this book. I try to cover the most elemental concepts found in Xamarin.Forms, taking one subject at a time. If you've liked this book but need some more spoken instructions, you can go over to `https://gur.codes` and check it out. The videos are hosted on YouTube, it would be great if you'd subscribe there and like the videos. If you still have any questions, please comment on the videos or reach out to me some other way. This can be done through Twitter at `https://twitter.com/jfversluis` or e-mail via `gerald@verslu.is`.

Another great resource for asking questions is *StackOverflow* (see `https://stackoverflow.com`). I am pretty active there as well. Working with Xamarin gives you a great advantage when searching on StackOverflow and on the Internet as a whole. Because the traditional Xamarin code is a projection of its native counterparts—Objective-C/Swift and Java—most of the time, you can take some Objective-C code, paste it into a project, add some semicolons, and you're good to go! There are many more relevant search results for you now that you can combine multiple programming languages.

© Gerald Versluis 2017

G. Versluis, *Xamarin.Forms Essentials*, https://doi.org/10.1007/978-1-4842-3240-8_10

There are also more formal ways to start learning Xamarin and Xamarin.Forms. There is an official Xamarin University. You can enroll in the university and follow live classes through the Internet. There are also some self-guided classes, but most of them are led by an instructor who is talking right then and there and available for questions. This is pretty awesome!

When you have chosen to learn with Xamarin University, you can also get certified. By following a special set of classes and passing a test, you can call yourself an official Xamarin Certified Developer.

Find more detail on this at `https://www.xamarin.com/university`.

Less official, but very good nonetheless, is the web site by Adam Pedley at `https://xamarinhelp.com/`. His blog is full of all kinds of Xamarin-related posts and is read by thousands of people every day. The topics are very helpful and range from beginner to advanced developers. Recently, he introduced a paid video course, to be found at `https://training.xamarinhelp.com/`. This is also a great resource to start after finishing this book. Not only will you get access to the video content, you will also be able to ask Adam questions directly on the Slack that he introduced for this. If something wasn't clear in the video, you can ask him right there and share your experience with others.

Just before finishing this book, check out this great post by Xamarin, which also focuses on the Xamarin.Forms learning curve. You can read it at `https://blog.xamarin.com/xamarin-forms-tips-beating-learning-curve/`.

Thank you very much for reading my book; I hope you found it useful!

Index

© Gerald Versluis 2017
G. Versluis, *Xamarin.Forms Essentials*, https://doi.org/10.1007/978-1-4842-3240-8

Get the eBook for only $5!

Why limit yourself?

With most of our titles available in both PDF and ePUB format, you can access your content wherever and however you wish—on your PC, phone, tablet, or reader.

Since you've purchased this print book, we are happy to offer you the eBook for just $5.

To learn more, go to http://www.apress.com/companion or contact support@apress.com.

Apress®